Stephen M Ostrander, Alexander Black

A History of the City of Brooklyn

Stephen M Ostrander, Alexander Black

A History of the City of Brooklyn

ISBN/EAN: 9783743312425

Manufactured in Europe, USA, Canada, Australia, Japa

Cover: Foto ©ninafisch / pixelio.de

Manufactured and distributed by brebook publishing software (www.brebook.com)

Stephen M Ostrander, Alexander Black

A History of the City of Brooklyn

A HISTORY

OF THE

CITY OF BROOKLYN

AND

KINGS COUNTY

BY

STEPHEN M. OSTRANDER, M. A.

LATE MEMBER OF THE HOLLAND SOCIETY, THE LONG ISLAND HISTORICAL
SOCIETY, AND THE SOCIETY OF OLD BROOKLYNITES

EDITED, WITH INTRODUCTION AND NOTES, BY

ALEXANDER BLACK

AUTHOR OF "THE STORY OF OHIO," ETC.

IN TWO VOLUMES

VOLUME I.

BROOKLYN

𝔓𝔲𝔟𝔩𝔦𝔰𝔥𝔢𝔡 𝔟𝔶 𝔖𝔲𝔟𝔰𝔠𝔯𝔦𝔭𝔱𝔦𝔬𝔫

1894

Copyright, 1894,
By ANNIE A. OSTRANDER.

All rights reserved.

This Edition is limited to Five Hundred
Copies, of which this is No. 21

PREFACE

At the time of his death, in 1885, Mr. Ostrander had completed considerable MS. for a history of the City of Brooklyn and Kings County; had prepared many chronological notes with a view to fuller writing, and had accumulated a mass of material in the form of transcripts, references, newspaper and other reports. It was his own understanding that a first volume of a proposed two-volume history might be regarded as well in hand, and that the wherewithal for the remaining chapters was advanced toward completion.

At the outset of his undertaking the editor met the embarrassment of not finding any outline which might reveal the precise form in which the author intended to cast his work. Mr. Ostrander worked with a definite idea, but did not formulate this idea in writing, and only the completed expressions of this idea remained for the guidance of the editor. It became apparent that the author intended to rearrange and extend the matter for the earlier chapters. This matter was preserved in the form of a series of articles published in the Brooklyn "Eagle," during 1879-80, covering the period from the discovery by Hudson to the beginning of the Revolution. The degree of attention which these articles attracted induced Mr. Ostrander to extend the series far beyond the range he originally intended to give to them. As a result these articles were not precisely consecutive, nor was the matter so ordered as to adapt itself to book chapters without material changes. Without knowing the author's design in detail, it was exceedingly difficult to effect these changes save upon lines which the natural symmetry of such a work seemed to suggest, and the editor has had no hesitation in so rearranging the material, and in changing such features of the narrative as had been temporarily essential to serial publication.

For the middle period, extending from the opening of the Revolution to the time of the consolidation of Brooklyn, Williamsburgh, and Bushwick, the author left a full narrative, and considerable collateral material. Beyond this point the chapters were in an unfinished sketch. In putting together the elements of this part of the work, the editor has been actuated by a wish to follow, so far as it might be apparent, the author's aim and plan. Possibly there is no occasion to offer apology for those passages in the body of the work, and particularly in the last chapter on modern Brooklyn, in which the editor has carried the narrative beyond the date of Mr. Ostrander's death. The few instances in which this occurs are obviously justified by the exigencies of the work. Nor should there be need for any defense on the part of the editor for the proportions of different elements of the work as now presented. No two historical writers would agree as to essential proportions in such a matter, and, without consultation with the author, no editor could hope to do more than compromise between such intent as appeared in unfinished work before him, and such ideal as to himself seemed wise.

Both author and editor have incurred obligations to Stiles's histories of Brooklyn and Kings County; to the "Notes" of Furman; Field's "Historic Scenes"; the Collections of the Long Island Historical Society; the histories of Thompson and Prime, and to other authorities to whom acknowledgment is offered in the notes and in the body of the work. The editor is indebted to the excellent alma-

nacs of the "Eagle" and of the "Citizen";
to the "Brooklyn Compendium," compiled by
John Dykeman, Jr., and published by order of
the Common Council in 1870; to the recent
compilation, "The Eagle and Brooklyn," edited by Henry W. B. Howard and Arthur N.
Jervis; and to various local reports and publications which do not call for enumeration
here.

A. B.

BROOKLYN, N. Y., *March* 5, 1894.

CONTENTS

STEPHEN M. OSTRANDER xi
                                           PAGE

CHAPTER I

THE REGION OF BROOKLYN AT THE TIME OF THE DISCOVERY

Geology and Conformation of Long Island. Evidences of the Glacial Period. Theory of the Glacial Action. "Back-Bone" of the Island. Earliest Historical Description. Trees. Animal Life. Indian Tribes: Their Subjugation by the Iroquois; Habits and Habitations . 1

CHAPTER II

DISCOVERY AND FIRST SETTLEMENTS

Early Voyagers. Henry Hudson. Attitude of Holland and Spain. Motives of Holland. Hudson's Reports. West India Company. Dutch on Manhattan Island. The Walloons and the Wallabout. Derivation of the Name Wallabout. First authentically recorded Settlements on Long Island. The Van Corlaer Purchase. Bennett and Bentyn's Purchase. Joris Jansen de Rapalje. Van Twiller. West India Company's Purchases on Long Island. East River Lands 16

CHAPTER III

THE INDIANS AND THE EARLY SETTLERS

The Dutch Policy toward the Indians. Puritan and Dutch Policy contrasted. Long Island Indians: Their Relations with the Whites. Kieft's Attacks on Pavonia and Corlaer's Hook. Uprising on Long Island. Overtures for Peace. Mission to Rockaway of De Vries and Olfertsen. Restoration of Friendly Relations . . 42

CHAPTER IV

THE BEGINNINGS OF BREUCKELEN
1643-1647

The Ferry and the Ferry Road. Settlement of Flatlands. Flatbush. Lady Deborah Moody and the Settlement of Gravesend. Early Settlements. The Name of Breuckelen. Henry C. Murphy's Comments. First Schepens and Schout. Commission from the Colonial Council. The Removal of Kieft. Arrival of Stuyvesant 53

CHAPTER V

DOMESTIC AND SOCIAL LIFE UNDER THE DUTCH
1647-1664

Beginning of Stuyvesant's Administration. Condition of the Colony. Character of the Early Dutch Houses. Household Arrangement. Dress. Funerals. Marriages. The Mixture of Races. Slavery. Religion. Attitude of Stuyvesant toward Sects other than Dutch Reformed. Triumph of Liberal Ideas. First Churches in Kings County. Troubles over the Church Tax. First Schools. The Dutch and Popular Education. End of Dutch Rule 69

CHAPTER VI

KINGS COUNTY AFTER THE ENGLISH CONQUEST
1665-1700

Assembly at Hempstead. The "Duke's Laws." Lovelace. New York retaken by the Dutch. Colve becomes Governor. return of English Rule under the Treaty of 1674. Dongan and the Popular Assembly. De Sille. Journal of Dankers and Sluyter. The Ferry. A Dutch Dinner. The Schoolmaster and the Constable.

CONTENTS

William and Mary and the Leisler Revolution. Sloughter appointed Governor. Execution of Leisler, and Subsequent Honors of a Public Reinterment. Long Island receives the name of Nassau. Development of Privateering. Captain Kidd visits and buries Treasure on Long Island. Bellomont and the Suppression of Piracy. First Trial for Treason 106

CHAPTER VII

BROOKLYN BEFORE THE REVOLUTION

1701-1775

Brooklyn becomes the Largest Long Island Settlement. Division of the Common Lands. Regulations as to the Cutting of Lumber. The King's Highway laid out. Brooklyn Officials at the Opening of the Century. Lord Cornbury's Proclamation to Long Island Justices. Slavery. Encroachments on the Common Highway. The Trial of Zenger. Population in 1738. Fortifying Long Island. Newspaper Glimpses of pre-Revolutionary Life. Ferries. Kings County in the Assembly and the Provincial Convention. Philip Livingston. General Town Meeting in Brooklyn 157

CHAPTER VIII

KINGS COUNTY DURING THE REVOLUTION

1775-1783

Kings County at the Opening of the Revolution. Participation in Events leading to the Crisis. Military Officers. Long Island Tories. The Continental and Provincial Congresses. Fortifying. Declaration of Independence. General Greene on Long Island. Draft in Kings County. Landing of the British at Gravesend. The Battle of Brooklyn. The Night Retreat. British Occupation of the County. Temptations to Disloyalty toward the American Cause, and Action of the People under British Pressure. The County in Congress. Losses in the Battle. Incidents. Prisoners billeted on the Inhabitants of Kings County. Long Island Refugees. Conspicuous Figures of the Period. Peace 211

LIST OF ILLUSTRATIONS

VOLUME I

PORTRAIT OF STEPHEN M. OSTRANDER . *Frontispiece*
THE FIRST BROOKLYN FERRY . . . . *Facing page* 38
THE FERRY IN 1746 102
BROOKLYN CHURCH AND DUFFIELD HOUSE IN 1776.
   (Drawn from Illustrations in Stiles's History of
   Brooklyn) 174
FIRST FIRE ENGINE USED IN BROOKLYN. (Drawn from
   lithographic illustration in Manual of the Common
   Council, 1863) 206
BROOKLYN DURING THE REVOLUTIONARY WAR. (From
   the Map by Gen. Jeremiah Johnson) 260

STEPHEN M. OSTRANDER

THE name of Stephen M. Ostrander has been honored in the city of Brooklyn as that of a man whose career exemplified a stainless citizenship. The honors have been not those of public favor offered in a citizen's lifetime, nor of memorials after he has passed away, but the monuments of a cherished memory, the recognition of a generous and wholesome personality.

Stephen M. Ostrander was born February 3, 1832, in the city of Brooklyn. He was of Dutch stock, his earliest ancestor in this country being Pieter Ostrander, who came to America in 1659. When Pieter Ostrander reached America with his wife and three children — a son, Pieter Pieterszen,[1] and two daughters, Tryutje and Geertje — Peter Stuyvesant was Governor of New Amsterdam, and the settlement on Manhattan Island occupied a small patch of land on the southern point of the land now occupied by the vast metropolis of New York. Settlers had been living on the Brooklyn side of the East River for a

[1] See appendix in second volume for explanation of system of Dutch family names.

little more than twenty years, and the Indians were still a formidable obstacle to the peace of the struggling young communities. Dutch immigration had not yet been checked by that bloodless conquest of the British, which five years later transformed New Amsterdam from a Dutch to an English colony, and changed its name to New York.

We afterward find Pieter Pieterszen living at Kingston. This second Pieter among the American Ostranders was born at Amsterdam, Holland, in 1650, and before coming to this country with his father had been enrolled as a cadet in the army of the Dutch king. In 1679 he married Rebecca, daughter of William Janszen Traphagen and Joostje Willems Van Northwyck. Among the children from this marriage was Hendrick Ostrander, born at New Hurley, N. Y., in 1693. Hendrick acquired the ownership of two thousand acres of land at Plattskill, which were evenly divided among his ten children. He was "a staunch adherent of the Reformed Dutch Church,"[1] and served in the army previous to the Revolution. His marriage to Elizabeth Van Bommel, of Kingston, took place in 1724. His son Christoffer, born and died at Plattskill, was the father of Stephen Ostrander, born at Poughkeepsie in 1769, and afterwards of Pompton Plains and Brunswick, N. J., who

[1] *American Ancestry*, vol. v., 1890.

was an eloquent minister of the Dutch Church. An illustration of the conditions prevailing at this period is offered by the fact that Stephen Ostrander preached in both English and Dutch.

The clerical Ostrander, who made an interesting reputation as a preacher in the early part of the present century, married Maria Duryea in 1796. His son, Abraham Duryea Ostrander, born at Pompton Plains in the following year, came to New York in his twelfth year, and began an energetic business career. From his earliest years he was of a studious tendency, and his self-acquired learning gave him an excellent mental equipment. He became a ripe scholar and influential citizen. For many years he led the first Sunday school in the Reformed Dutch Church of Brooklyn (corner of William and Fulton streets), walking to the meeting-place from his home at Flatbush. In 1820, he married Margaret T. Wilson, daughter of Peter Wilson, LL. D., of Columbia College, the tutor of Charles Anthon and other well-known scholars, and distinguished for having drawn up the constitution of the State of New Jersey.

Abraham Duryea Ostrander's three sons were Peter Wilson, George A., and Stephen M. Ostrander. George A. Ostrander, a graduate of Columbia College and of the College of Physicians and Surgeons, was the first house surgeon of the Long Island College Hospital. The other two brothers became lawyers, and it is among the interesting traditions of the Kings County bar that they were frequently in opposition in the same case. Under such circumstances their professional steel clashed brilliantly, but the firm affection between the brothers had no hint of strife or rivalry.

Stephen M. Ostrander, born 1831, was educated in this city and at Columbia College. He was admitted to the bar and began the practice of law while a decidedly young man, but soon made his personality felt in the life of the city. If his tastes led him to a studious life at home, his gifts and ambitions drew him into those features of political activity which demand voice as well as counsel. He championed the Democratic party, and until the close of his life he spoke his loyalty in no uncertain tones. He became one of the "war horses" of the party in campaign times, and was a respected adviser in those political times of peace when parties prepare for war. He would have made an admirable public servant, but party conditions did not bring him to the front as a candidate, though they welcomed his voice on the platform. He wished to be surrogate, but the nomination he sought was given to Jacob I. Bergen. He was not an insistent candidate within his party, and the rewards which might reasonably be considered to have belonged to him had not been bestowed at the time of his death.

As a lawyer, Mr. Ostrander was conscientious, painstaking, forcible. His genial personality made him popular wherever he appeared. His strong figure fitted his character, which was staunch and equable. By temperament he was inclined to see the whimsical side of things, while quick to exclude any element of this sort from matters commanding his serious thought.

Stories concerning him reveal his quick humor. One day a witty but not especially well-versed Irish lawyer called upon him for assistance in preparing a case. One point of perplexity with the inquirer was as to the motive power on the ferries before the use of steam. Knowing Ostrander's familiarity with early Brooklyn history, the inquiring lawyer demanded information as to this point. "Before the days of steam," said Ostrander, "they used to have horse boats." "Horse boats?" queried the lawyer, with a look of continued perplexity. "Yes." "Did the horses swim ahead of them?" "No," solemnly returned Ostrander, "they had four holes cut in the bottom of the boat; the horse's legs passed through these holes, permitting him to walk on the bottom, and thus propel the boat." "Good!" said the listener, "I'll win the case." And he did.

Mr. Ostrander's interest in American history was perhaps a natural result of his ancestry and his tendencies as a student. He early began the accumulation of historical material, and finally formed a definite plan for writing a history of the city of Brooklyn and Kings County. He was an active member of the Society of Old Brooklynites, frequently addressing that body, and as a member of the Long Island Historical Society, — in whose handsome hall, on Pierrepont Street, he was the first to lecture under the auspices of the society, — he found many opportunities to further his hobby of historical investigation. He also entered that fraternity of descendants of Dutch stock, the Holland Society of New York.

During the later years of his life he was a frequent contributor to the newspapers and local magazines, generally upon topics directly related to local history. Debated questions as to historical matters always interested him, and his pen was ever ready with a casual comment. He was a good debater, though not pugnacious, and never an ungenerous opponent. In his profession, in his political associations, in his relations with his fellow-citizens and with fellow-members of the different societies to which he was attracted, he was always well poised, highly respected, uniformly welcomed. His catholic tastes and sympathies gave him many interests, as they gave him many friends. It was as natural that he should be prominent in the Presbyterian Church, which he attended, as that he should be a leading figure in the Masonic fraternity, to which he was proud to own allegiance. His commanding figure, good voice, and easy manner made him a popular speaker on social as well as public occasions.

Mr. Ostrander married Annie A. Hammond on August 7, 1866. His domestic relations were in keeping with the fine symmetry of his character. No marriage could have been happier. In the preparation of the historical work which was incomplete when his short illness closed his life, he had the loyal appreciation and assistance of his wife.

He died on November 19, 1885. The extent of his practice and income might have indicated the probability of a considerable fortune, but he was too open-handed to have become a rich man. He died worth a good name.

HISTORY OF BROOKLYN

CHAPTER I

THE REGION OF BROOKLYN AT THE TIME OF THE DISCOVERY

Geology and Conformation of Long Island. Evidences of the Glacial Period. Theory of the Glacial Action. "Back-Bone" of the Island. Earliest Historical Description. Trees. Animal Life. Indian Tribes: Their Subjugation by the Iroquois; Habits and Habitations.

THE geology of Long Island has always been regarded as a particularly interesting theme for those concerned in the study of such matters, since the examination of its phases brings into view so many and such various points of speculative interest. Prime in his "History of Long Island"[1] remarks that "when we consider the retired situation of Long Island, and how little it has excited the notice of travelers, it is not surprising that its

[1] *A History of Long Island, from its First Settlement by Europeans, to the year 1845, with Special Reference to its Ecclesiastical Concerns.* By Nathaniel S. Prime. 1845.

geological character as well as other peculiarities should have remained so long unexplored. Until quite recently very few scientific men have even deigned to give it a passing notice, though the assertion may be safely hazarded that scarcely any other tract of land of equal extent on the American Continent furnishes more abundant room for the *imagination* of geologists to play upon, or that imposes a stronger necessity for *conjecturing* the operation of some tremendous agency, which in its freaks had invaded the domains of both the land and the ocean, and after completing its sport had silently retired without leaving a track to determine its origin or identify its form."

The geologist of the present day does not seem to regard the field as one calling in the same degree for the exercise of the imagination, though the more definite knowledge acquired and made familiar since the time of the publication just quoted has in one sense vastly extended the opportunity for speculation. Certainly it no longer can be said that scientific men have neglected the investigation of the subject.

Commenting on the investigations of Dr. Dwight, Prime says:—

"From all these considerations, the inference has been regarded as legitimate that Long Island was once through its whole extent attached to the main; and some powerful agency, the form of which is now left entirely to conjecture, forced the separation which is now marked by the intervening Sound. One of the most plausible suppositions is that the separation has been effected by some resistless torrent of water, which, under peculiar circumstances that it is impossible now to determine, has swept out the intervening land, and left its channel to be occupied by the waters of the ocean."

Thus vaguely were the early speculations set forth. With a well developed glacial theory to aid him the modern geologist is able to present a fairly circumstantial picture of probable conditions in the past. We now know with reasonable certainty that Brooklyn rests on soil that is a monument to a vast force quite different from any that were included in the hesitating speculations of the early writers.

In an admirable review of the subject written by Charles M. Skinner we are presented with a picturesque outline of the glacial theory. We are reminded that Brooklyn stands on rubble that was rolled down from the New England mountains to the northward by a glacier larger than the combined areas of all the glaciers now existing on the earth. How many thousands of years ago this great glacier began its work we may only guess within somewhat liberal margins. This continent of ice covered the whole of the northern part of North America, burying mountains beneath its bulk and hollowing the beds of the great fresh-water seas that Chicago and its sister cities front upon to-day, burying, too, for aught we know, the remains of civilizations, though nothing at present has been taken out of the glacial drift, except rude stone implements, to show what the probable condition of man was at that time.

This ice lay so deep that not even Mount Washington barred its advance, and to-day geologists find the summit of this mountain heaped with blocks of stone that were dragged from other points and left there when the ice melted; for glaciers are not stationary, like ice on ponds and marshes, but have an onward movement toward their point of melting that varies, with the slope of their beds, from six to thirty-six inches a day. In Greenland the whole interior is covered with ice thousands of feet thick, the movement of which is hindered by a wall of mountains that nearly surrounds that island, but wherever a valley opens a way for it the ice sends down a tongue to the sea, and from these tongues the ocean currents break off the icebergs that float down the Atlantic. In their descent these glaciers act as plows, wearing off so much earth and rock from the hills that the icebergs are freighted with them, and where they melt their stony burdens sink to the bottom of the sea, forming the Grand Banks of Newfoundland.

The ice that buried upper North America acted in the same manner as the Greenland ice to-day: it eroded the mountains, it sent off bergs, and the rocks and gravel that it tore from the hills by a pressure of a thousand tons to the square yard were dropped at its foot, where they formed a moraine, as it is called. These moraines, which may be seen at the feet of the glaciers in Switzerland and British Columbia, and that sometimes make heaps and hills of rock, like rude forts, forty and fifty feet high, are trifling affairs to the shoals left by the great glacier of the ice age, for that can be traced from the Atlantic coast nearly to the Mississippi River. Long Island, measuring approximately 120 miles in length, is a small part of the dump of this glacier, and it is sometimes possible to tell where the stones came from that are found on the surface. For example, there are in Brooklyn anthophyllite from Westchester county, feldspar and green mica from Fort George, basalt from the Palisades of the Hudson, and a block of labradorite was found on Myrtle Avenue that had been carried down from the Adirondacks, three hundred miles.

The members of the United States geological survey, supported by the New York and other state surveys, have studied into the course and volume of the glacier and mapped its moraine from Montauk Point westward nearly half across the continent. By this survey we learn that the gneiss that crosses under the East River and approaches the surface at Astoria, is the only bed rock to be found on Long Island, Brooklyn resting on a cushion of glacial drift that in some places is three hundred feet deep. Originally there were cliffs of gneiss edging the Atlantic, but the great glacier shaved these down to mere ledges. Central Park, New York, preserves a number of these ledges, rounded off into "sheep backs" and scratched by the pieces of stone that formed a grinding surface to the under side of the ice, while every now and then a boulder comes to the top of the ground in Brooklyn that is scored and almost polished by rubbing against those ledges. Pieces from that very outcrop in Hell Gate are found in Brooklyn streets.

We are also reminded in Mr. Skinner's review that manufacturers of brick, tile, terra cotta, pottery, and porcelain in other states have to rely in part on the clay beds that environ Brooklyn for their material, and, in fact, that clay and sand are the only economic mineral products of Long Island. The explanation of this is that Brooklyn clays are rich in silica, which is apt to be deficient in the clays of New Jersey. Without silica the clays are weak, and bricks and utensils made from them readily crack and crumble; but by mixing properly the best results are obtained. Excellent sand for glass-making is also found in and near Brooklyn.

There are many evidences in support of the theory that since the completion of the great glacier's work the surface of Long Island has subsided considerably. A recent writer[1] on the geology of Long Island says:

"The shore at the west end of the island

[1] Richard M. Bayles, in *Long Island Magazine*, September, 1893.

has also undergone decided changes — even within the memory of persons now living. Personal witnesses have testified that about the first of this century Coney Island was composed of high and extensive sand hills, which have since been flattened down to a low beach, sometimes covered by the tides. About the same time salt meadow-grass was annually cut on a part of the beach now far out into the ocean. We are also informed that cedar-trees were cut for fence-posts, and other timber for firewood, about 150 years ago, on land which is now submerged by the ocean a mile and a half or two miles from the shore. There was also a house standing upon what was known as Pine Island, the site of which is now beneath the breakers, at a considerable distance from the present shore."

Within the range of Kings County a stratum of salt meadow has been found at a depth of one hundred and twenty feet, and at other points within the county shells have been found fifty and sixty feet below the surface. What is generally called the "back-bone of Long Island" is a ridge of low hills beginning at the western end within the limits of Kings County and running almost the whole length of the Island. Of the boulders or erratic blocks found on the Island in this central range of hills and between them and the north shore, Mr. Bayles writes: —

" The boulders or erratic blocks found upon the Island are mostly met with on the central range of hills and between them and the north shore. They are often contained in a stratum which is interstratified with deposits of sand, clay, and gravel, and is often exposed along the coast. Some of the blocks, when first disinterred, exhibit scratches upon one or more of their sides. Rocks of the same constituent formation are found in Rhode Island, Connecticut, and along the Hudson River. And those of the Island, in their variations, correspond so accurately with the rocks of the localities mentioned that it seems probable that they came from those localities. For example, the boulders on the east end are like the granite, gneiss, mica slate, green-stone, and sienite of Rhode Island and the east part of Connecticut; opposite New London and the mouth of the Connecticut River are boulders like the granites, gneiss, and hornblende rock of those localities; opposite New Haven are found the red sandstone and conglomerate, fissile and micaceous red sandstone, trap conglomerate, compact trap, amygdaloid and verd antique; opposite Black Rock are the granites, gneiss, hornblende, quartz, and white limestone, like those in Fairfield County; and from

Huntington to Brooklyn, hornblende, crystalline lime-stone, trap, red sandstone, gneiss, and granite, are the same in appearance as those found in the vicinity of the Hudson River."

The earliest historical description of Long Island, in Daniel Denton's "A Brief Description of New York, formerly called New Amsterdam," published in London in 1670, remarks that "the greatest part of the Island is very full of timber, as Oaks, white and red, Walnut-trees, Chestnut-trees, which yield stores of Mast, etc." The same record says:

"For wild beast there is Deer, Bear, Wolves, Foxes, Raccoons, Otters, Musquashes, and Skunks. Wild fowl there is a great store of, as Turkeys, Heath-hens, Quails, Partridges, Pigeons, Cranes, Geese of several sorts, Brants, Widgeons, Teal, and divers others. Upon the south side of Long Island in the winter lie store of Whales and Grampusses, which the inhabitants begin with small boats to make a trade, catching to their no small benefit. Also, an innumerable multitude of seals, which make an excellent oyle; they lie all the winter upon some broken Marshes and Beaches or bars of sand before mentioned, and might be easily got were there some skilful men would undertake it."

Prime (1845) mentions the "remarkable fact

in the natural history of this small territory, that of all the *land-birds* belonging to the United States, either as resident or migratory, two thirds of them are to be found on Long Island; of the *water-birds* a still larger proportion."

It is estimated that at the time of its discovery representatives of thirteen different Indian tribes occupied Long Island. The region of Kings County was occupied by the Canarsie tribe, which included the Nyacks at New Utrecht, the Marechawicks at Brooklyn, and the Jamecos at Jamaica. The headquarters of the tribe was in the vicinity of modern Canarsie. From the names of the other tribes scattered over the Island — the Rockaways, Montauks, Merricks, Manhassets, Patchogues, Shinnecocks, etc. — many of the town and village names of the Island are drawn. The names Paumanacke and Seawanhacka have been applied both to the grand sachems elected by all the Indian tribes and to the Island itself, which has also been given the title of Wamponomon.

The last mentioned name was evidently suggested by the fact that the chief business of the tribes in this region was the making of *wampum*, the shell-money of the Indians, and an article of manufacture for ornamental purposes also. The Island was rich in shells, and these were ground, polished, pierced for stringing. In the earlier tradings for land the red men were eager to get *runxes*, a brad awl with which they pierced the shell. They made various forms of earthenware for domestic purposes; their war implements were often of admirable workmanship; and their canoes were of a size and strength demanded by the hazards of the journeys they undertook upon sea and Sound.

"In regard to their religion," says Prime, "the Long Island Indians were polytheists and idolaters. Besides the good and the evil spirit, to each of which they seemed to ascribe supreme power, they had a god for each of the four corners of the earth, the four seasons of the year, the others of the elements of nature, the productions of the earth, the vicissitudes of day and night, besides a number of domestic deities. The good deity they called *Cauhlantoowut*, and the evil spirit was named *Mutcheshesumetook;* to both of which they paid homage and offered sacrifices. They had small idols or images which, they supposed, were acquainted with the will of the gods, and made it known to the *pawwaws*, or priests. These possessed unbounded influence, from their supposed intercourse with the gods and knowledge of their will. Their religious festivals were attended with the most violent gesticulations and horrible yells, as well as other disorders. They firmly believed in a future state of existence, in a far distant country to the west, where the brave and good would enjoy themselves eternally in singing, feasting, hunting, and dancing; while the coward and traitor, the thief and liar, would be eternally condemned to servile labor — so much despised by the Indian — which in its results should be attended with endless disappointment. The dead were buried in all their personal attire, and, if warriors, in their arms. The body was placed in a sitting posture, and after being covered up, a bowl of *scaump* (pounded corn) was placed on the grave to support the occupant on his imagined journey. The period of mourning continued a full year, the close of which was celebrated with a feast, accompanied with dancing that continued from the setting to the rising of the sun. It was a peculiar custom of this singular people never to mention the names of their departed friends after their remains were deposited in tombs, and it was regarded as an insult if repeated by others. Every wigwam in which death occurred was immediately demolished, and a new one, if needed, erected in its stead."

The wigwams of the Indians were designed

each to accommodate a number of families, the bark-covered frame being of eighteen to twenty feet in width, and a length of one hundred and fifty feet or more, as might be required by the number of the families that were to occupy it. An opening at the ridge gave escape to the smoke from the family fires.

The Long Island Indians, notwithstanding the strength which might be presumed to have resulted from their insular position, were under the rule of the masters on the continent. The tribes to the east yielded to the New England Pequods. The Canarsies bowed to the majestic despotism of the Iroquois.[1]

Under the species of "protection" enforced by the Iroquois, the Canarsies were obliged to pay regular tribute for the privilege of being unmolested, and much of this tax was doubtless paid in wampum. The collection of this tax seems at the time of the first white settlements to have been intrusted to the Mohawks, who were members of the confederacy. When the tax was due it had to be delivered, or the

---

[1] At the time of the discovery the Iroquois, or League of the Five Nations, claimed to have subdued and mastered all the Indian tribes from the Atlantic to the Mississippi. The Iroquois occupied in particular the middle and upper region of New York State. The earliest of the general histories of this remarkable confederacy was written by Cadwallader Colden, who died on Long Island in 1776.

debtors were likely to hear from headquarters. Samuel Jones, writing in 1817, says [1] that there is no evidence that the Indians on Long Island, eastward of about thirty miles from New York, were tributary to the Five Nations; and adds that "we have no reason to believe that the Five Nations had any war with the Indians on Long Island after it was settled by Europeans." Furman [2] regards this statement as extraordinary, and offers evidence of the fact that farmers coming to New York city in the fall of the year from the east end of Long Island, during the early period of settlement, brought with them quantities of wampum to be forwarded as tribute to the Iroquois masters at Albany. It has frequently been claimed by historical writers that the consistory of the Dutch Church at Albany were for many years the agents for the receipt of tribute from the Montauks and other Indians on the eastern end of Long Island, which, if a fact, was, as we shall see, entirely consistent with the conservative attitude of the Dutch pioneers.

[1] *New York Historical Society's Collections*, vol. iii. p. 324.
[2] *Antiquities of Long Island*, p. 29.

CHAPTER II

DISCOVERY AND FIRST SETTLEMENTS

Early Voyagers. Henry Hudson. Attitude of Holland and Spain. Motives of Holland. Hudson's Reports. West India Company. Dutch on Manhattan Island. The Walloons and the Wallabout. Derivation of the Name Wallabout. First authentically recorded Settlements on Long Island. The Van Corlaer Purchase. Bennett and Bentyn's Purchase. Joris Jansen de Rapalje. Van Twiller. West India Company's Purchases on Long Island. East River Lands.

IT is possible that in the voyages of the Cabots, Long Island was sighted if not touched; and the voyage of Esteben Gomez in 1524, "to find a way to Cathay," may leave the same possibility. There is every probability that the Spaniard, Giovanni da Verrazano, who in 1524 made a voyage to this country in the interest of France, — the first official French exploration in this direction, — entered New York harbor. From the account of this mariner it appears likely that he skirted the coast of Long Island, saw Block Island, giving to it the name of Louisa, mother of Francis I., and anchored in the harbor of Newport.

Those who care to speculate as to possible visitors early in the sixteenth century, may take account also of the voyage of Lucas Vasquez de Aillon and Matienzo, made in 1526.

That one at least of the early Spanish voyagers, all of whom were looking for a passage to India, had seen the region of the coast on which Long Island lies, is indicated by the presence in England of a map which was in existence before Henry Hudson made his first voyage. In this map the name Rio de San Antonio is given to the river afterward named after Hudson.

This being the case it is not to be considered as certain, if it is to be considered as likely, that Henry Hudson really sailed across the Atlantic with any idea of finding either a northwest passage to India, or in hope of finding somewhere under 40° north latitude any passage to the western ocean.

Why Henry Hudson should formally have pretended to seek such a passage will appear from a glance at the political situation at the time of his voyage.

When Hudson left Europe, Holland and Spain were at swords' points. Carlyle has pithily summed up the case: " Those Dutch are a stirring people. They raised their land out of a marsh, and went on for a long period of time herding cows and making cheese, and might have gone on with their cows and cheese till doomsday. But Spain comes and says, 'We want you to believe in St. Ignatius.' 'Very sorry,' replied the Dutch, 'but we can't.' 'God! but you *must*,' says Spain; and they went about with guns and swords to make the Dutch believe in St. Ignatius. Never made them believe in him, but did succeed in breaking their own vertebral column forever, and raising the Dutch into a great nation."

The Dutch were well acquainted with the work of the Spanish explorers, and the idea of contesting with Spain for a share in the profits and advantages of transatlantic discovery grew out of the war with Spain. At this time international law gave to a sovereign any new land discovered in his name, and not already laid hold upon by any Christian prince. If Holland was to fight Spain in America it would be useful to have at least the shadow of a tenable international claim; and so Hudson ignored the earlier Spanish voyages in assuming to discover the river to which his name was given, and the land thereabouts which the Dutch, with beautiful political audacity, first claimed to own by right of discovery, and afterward claimed to own through Spain as "first discoverer and founder of that New World."

The first proposition to make a Dutch expedition to America came from an Englishman, a sea captain named Beets. The States-General refused this offer, but jealousy of Spain's resources in the New World kept alive the ambitions of the Dutch and finally resulted in the formation of the West India Company.

The theory of this company was both commercial and political. The scheme was first broached by an exiled Antwerp merchant, William Usselinx, in 1592. Before it came to completion a Greenland Company came into existence, and, while feigning to hunt up a northwest passage, its ships are said to have sailed into the North River, and to have landed on these shores in 1598. It was not until 1606 that Usselinx's ideas were formulated in a working plan. The company might then have been fully formed had not talk of a peace with Spain made it politically unwise to risk the adventure.

When in 1609 Henry Hudson, the English sailor, who already had made several voyages across the Atlantic, offered his services to the West India Company, it was ostensibly to seek a passage to India. The Amsterdam chamber of the company fitted out Hudson in the "Half Moon," which sailed out of the Texel on April 4, 1609.

Whatever may have been Hudson's intentions as to any search for a northwest passage, he abandoned such a search in favor of one for a more southerly passage, having, it is said, been told by Captain John Smith "that there was a sea leading into the Western Ocean by the north of Virginia."

After landing at Newfoundland, at Penobscot Bay, and at Cape Cod, Hudson found Delaware Bay; but a week later, realizing that he was too far south, he steered the Half Moon into the "Great North River of New Netherland." It is the tradition that during the exploration of the great bay and river a boat's crew from the Half Moon made its first landing on Long Island, at the sandy shore of Coney Island; but there might seem to be a likelihood that a landing would be made further to the north.

The Long Island Indians whom Hudson met were representatives of the Canarsie tribe. These Indians visited the Half Moon without fear, and gladly welcomed the strangers, doubtless looking upon them with much awe.

Hudson says "they brought with them green tobacco to exchange for knives and other implements. They were clad in deerskins and expressed a wish to obtain a supply of European clothing." Some of them were decked in gay feathers and others in furs. Hudson refers to the stock of maize or Indian corn, "whereof they make good bread." It thus would appear that the Island had a good reputation two hundred and seventy years ago for corn, which it still maintains. They also had a good supply of hemp which they offered in trade, and must have understood its manufacture in a rude way.[1]

Hudson remarks, "that upon landing he saw a great store of men, women, and children, who gave them tobacco." In his account he describes the country "as being full of great tall oaks." He says "the lands were as pleasant with grass and flowers and goodly trees as ever they had seen, and very sweet smells came from them."

The pleasant relations between Hudson and the Indians did not continue very long. Hudson does not state how the difficulty arose, but one of his men was killed with an arrow

[1] Among Brooklyn's manufactures in recent years rope-making has taken a prominent place.

and two others wounded. The unfortunate man was buried on the point of Coney Island, which Hudson named Colman's Point, in honor of the dead seaman.

Hudson remained for a month, pursuing his explorations of the river which has since carried his name, and then set sail for Holland. The news which the explorer brought home was of a sort to arouse the interest of the Dutch people.

Hudson told of a rich region alive with fur-bearing animals, — an important circumstance to speculators in a cold country like that of Holland, where the question of warm clothing was always to the fore. The immediate result of Hudson's reports was the launching of many private ventures and an urgent movement to complete the organization of the West India Company. It was not until 1621 that the States-General at last signed the charter, and meanwhile traders had established themselves on Manhattan Island.

Although the English in Virginia were beginning to express their theories of claim to the Hudson region, the West India Company went into possession in 1623, sending as director, Adrien Jorissen Tienpont, who made stronger the fortification at Manhattan Island,

and built a new fortification near that placed by the advance guard of Dutch traders (in 1618) near Albany. This post was called Fort Orange.

Tienpont was succeeded in 1626 by Peter Minuit, who was not long in making a bargain with the Indians for the whole of Manhattan Island. The price paid was about twenty-four dollars.

In making this significant purchase Minuit and those whom he represented had in mind to make the Manhattan Island settlement the principal centre of trade and colonization, if anything like colonization may be said to have occupied the attention of the Dutch at the time. There was, indeed, a passage in the charter of 1621, by which the company was required "to advance the peopling of these fruitful and unsettled parts," but actual colonization was not a matter of much thought until the later exigencies of trade made the subject important. Followed as it was by the organization under a charter of a council with supreme executive, legislative, and judicial authority, the movement under Minuit is to be regarded as the foundation of the present state of New York.

It was shortly before the appointment of

Minuit as Director of New Netherland that a number of Walloons applied to Sir Dudley Carleton, principal Secretary of State to King Charles I., for permission to settle in Virginia.

"These Walloons," says Brodhead, "whose name was derived from their original 'Waal-sche' or French extraction, had passed through the fire of persecution. They inhabited the southern Belgic provinces of Hainault, Namur, Luxemburg, Limburg, and part of the ancient bishopric of Liège, and spoke the old French language. When the northern provinces of the Netherlands formed their political union at Utrecht, in 1579, the southern provinces, which were generally attached to the Romish Church, declined joining the confederation. Many of their inhabitants, nevertheless, professed the principles of the Reformation. Against these Protestant Walloons the Spanish government exercised the most rigid measures of inquisitorial vengeance, and the subjects of an unrelenting persecution emigrated by thousands into Holland, where they knew that strangers of every race and creed were sure of an asylum and a welcome. Carrying with them a knowledge of the arts, in which they were great proficients, they were distinguished in their new home for their tasteful and persevering industry. To the Walloons the Dutch were probably indebted for much of the repute which they gained as a nation in many branches of manufactures. Finding in Holland a free scope for their religious opinions, the Walloons soon introduced the public use of their church service, which to this day bears witness to the characteristic toleration and liberality of the Fatherland."

The Virginia company, whether for want of cordiality or other reason, did not attract the colonizing ardor of the Walloons, who turned to New Netherland, and a party of them came over with Minuit.

The lands first allotted to the Walloons were on Staten Island. It is possible that this situation seemed to the French exiles too remote from the protection of the Manhattan Island fort. However they may have been influenced, certain of the new-comers chose rather to settle at Fort Orange and others at that bend in the East River which has since been known as the Wallabout.

Various explanations of the name Wallabout have been offered. That of a derivation from *wahlebocht*, bay of the foreigners, has been favorably received; but Stiles[1] quotes

[1] *A History of the City of Brooklyn, including the Old Town and Village of Brooklyn, the Town of Bushwick, and the Village and City of Williamsburgh.* By Henry R. Stiles. 1867.

Samuel Alofsen [from the "Literary World," No. 68, May 20, 1848] as maintaining that the locality was named by the early Dutch settlers prior to the arrival of the Walloons; that the name is derived from *een waal*, basin of a harbor or inner harbor, and *een bogt*, a bend, and that, like its European namesake in the city of Amsterdam, it signifies "The Bend of the Inner Harbor."

Notwithstanding the indications which several writers have assumed to find of settlement at the Wallabout during or shortly after the year 1623, there is an absence of definite evidence of any actual settlement at any date so early, and probabilities are entirely against a settlement at that time so far from the fort. There were early hunting-lodges and temporary trading-houses incidental to the shooting and trading trips of those occupying the Manhattan Island settlement, and there is the possibility that unrecorded residence by the Walloons or others may have been established at the Wallabout before the recorded grants. But for definite evidence of a first settlement in the shape of an authoritative taking of land we must turn to the purchase by Jacob Van Corlaer in 1636.

Van Corlaer was an official under the

administration of the new Director of New Amsterdam, Van Twiller. The Director himself, who had been a clerk in the West India Company's office, had great eagerness for acquiring territory. He bought from the Indians a part of Connecticut, and planted near the present site of Hartford a fort, which he could not but understand would be a thorn in the side of the English. Not only did he freely spend the government's money in buying land and strengthening fortifications on a most ambitious plan, but he granted to himself and favored officials associated with him choice pieces of land on Manhattan Island, and across the river on Long Island. The year following the Van Corlaer grant, Van Twiller's conduct, which all but ruined the company, resulted in his recall, and the appointment of William Kieft as his successor.

At this time the settlement on Manhattan Island occupied only a very small region below the present Battery Place. Its main feature was the fort, whose protecting presence was one of the inducements which the Company extended to colonists. A decree issued in 1629 declared that any member of the West India Company who, under certain easy conditions, should form a settlement of not less than fifty persons, none of whom should be under fifteen years of age, should be granted a tract of land fronting sixteen miles upon the sea or upon any navigable river (or eight miles when both shores of the river were occupied), and extending thence inland indefinitely; and that the *patroons* to whom such grants of land should be made should exercise manorial rights over their estates.

The provisions were sufficiently liberal to assure the making of many minor settlements, and it was natural that many eyes should be turned toward the softly undulating country on the southeast of the East River. The official land-grabbing under Van Twiller retarded rather than advanced colonization. Indeed, the company scarcely fulfilled the obligations of the charter in sending colonists to the new region.

The grant to Van Corlaer appears as a purchase from the Indians of a "flat" of land called "Casteteeuw, on Sewan-hackey, or Long Island." The same date is given to grants to Andries Hudde and Wolfert Gerritsen of flats to the west of Van Corlaer's, Van Twiller himself getting the desirable land to the east.

These purchases, amounting to 15,000 acres, were in a level region, reported already to have been cultivated to some extent by the Indians, and appealing to men brought up in a flat country, and unaccustomed to wood-clearing, as superior to the regions having a heavy tree growth. Plows were soon at work, and from the settlement thus begun grew the village of "New Amersfoort," now the town of Flatlands.

In the same year (1636) the Indians sold to William Adriaense Bennett and Jacques Bentyn a tract of 930 acres at Gowanus, a region so named by the Indians. The tract extended from the vicinity of Twenty-eighth Street, along Gowanus Cove and the bay, to the New Utrecht line. The transaction is described in the following record:—

"On this 4th day of April (English style), 1677, appeared before me Michil Hainelle, acknowledged as duly installed Clerk and Secretary, certain persons, to wit: Zeuw Kamingh, otherwise known in his walks (or travels) as Kaus Hansen, and Keurom, both Indians, who, in presence of the undersigned witnesses, deposed and declared, that the limits or widest bounds of the land of Mr. Paulus Vanderbeeck, in the rear, has been or is a certain tree or stump on the Long Hill, on the one side, and on the other the end of the Indian foot-path, and that it extends to the creek of the third meadows, which land and ground, they further depose and declare, previous to the present time, was sold by a certain Indian, known as Chief or Sachem Ka, to Jacques Bentyn and William Adriaense (Bennett), the latter formerly the husband of Marie Thomas, now the wife of Mr. Paulus Vanderbeeck; which account they both maintain to be the truth, and truly set forth in this deposition.

"In witness of the truth is the original of this with the said Indians' own hands subscribed, to wit: By Zeuw Kamingh or Kaus Hansen, with this mark ( ) and by Kcurom with this mark ( ) in the presence of Lambert Dorlant, who by request signed his name hereto as a witness. Took place at Brookland on the day and date above written.

"Compared with the original and attested to be correct.
"MICHIL HAINELLE, *Clerk*."

Three years afterward Bentyn sold to Bennett all or nearly all of his share of the land acquired in this early sale.

The purchase by Bentyn and Bennett is to be regarded as the first exchange of property looking to a settlement within the limits of the present city of Brooklyn. It was in the following year that a second purchase was made by Joris Jansen de Rapalje, who was one of the Walloon emigrants who came over with Minuit in 1623. Rapalje's first residence after reaching this country was at Fort Orange (Albany). In 1626 he removed to New Amsterdam. In June, 1637, he bought a tract adjoining the Rennegackonk, a little Long Island stream entering the East River at "the bend of Marechkawieck," at the Wahlebocht or the present Wallabout. There were about 335 acres in the purchase, part of the land now being represented by the grounds of the Marine Hospital.

At this time Rapalje lived on the north side of the river road, now Pearl Street, and on the south side of the fort. Writing of this period Thomas A. Janvier says: —

"Actually, only two roads were established when the town of New Amsterdam was founded, and these so obviously were necessary that, practically, they established themselves. One of them, on the line of the present Stone and Pearl Streets, — the latter then the waterfront, — led from the Fort to the Brooklyn Ferry at about the present Peck Slip. The other, on the line of the present Broadway, led northward from the Fort, past farms and gardens falling away toward the North River, as far as the present Park Row; and along the line of that street, and of Chatham Street, and of the Bowery, went on into the wilderness. After the Palisade was erected, this road was known as far as the city gate (at Wall Street) as the Heere Straat, or High Street; and beyond the wall as the Heere Wegh — for more than a century the only highway that traversed the Island from end to end."

Rapalje followed the example of the colonists in general in snuggling close to the Fort. The writer just quoted remarks: —

"Upon the town rested continually the dread of an Indian assault. At any moment the hot-headed act of some angry colonist might easily bring on a war. In the early autumn of 1655, when peaches were ripe, an assault actually was made: being a vengeance against the whites because Hendrick Van Dyke had shot to death an Indian woman whom he found stealing peaches in his orchard (lying just south of the present Rector Street) on the North River shore. Fortunately, warning came to the townsfolk, and, crowding their women and children into the Fort, they were able to beat off the savages; whereupon the savages, being the more eager for revenge, fell upon the settlements about Pavonia and on Staten Island: where the price paid for Hendrick Van Dyke's peaches was the wasting of twenty-eight farms, the bearing away of one hundred and fifty Christians into captivity, and one hundred Christians outright slain."

During a part of the time that he lived in New Amsterdam Rapalje was an innkeeper. He appears to have been a man of the people, for in August, 1641, he was one of twelve men to represent Manhattan, Breuckelen, and Pavonia in considering measures necessary in dealing with the Indians. It was at about 1654 that he began living at the Wallabout. Certainly he lived on Long Island in 1655, for in that year he began serving as a magistrate in Breuckelen.

It once was customary to assert that Rapalje's daughter Sarah was the first white child born on Long Island. The fact is that Sarah Rapalje was born during the residence of her parents at Fort Orange. The error arose from the supposition that Rapalje settled at the Wallabout upon his arrival in this country in 1623. Of Sarah Rapalje, who may probably be said to have been the first white female child born in the New Netherland Colony, one of her descendants, the author of the History of the Bergen Family, says:

"The early historians of this State and locality, led astray by a petition presented by her, April 4th, 1656, (when she resided at the Walle-boght,) to the Governor and Council, for some meadows, in which she states that she is the 'first-born Christian child in New Netherlands,' assert that she was born at the Walle-boght. Judge Benson, in his writings, even ventures to describe the house where this took place. He says: 'On the point of land formed by the cove in Brooklyn, known as the Walle-boght, lying on its westerly side (it should have been *easterly*), was built the first house on Long Island, and inhabited by Joris Jansen de Rapalje, one of the first white settlers on the Island, and in which was born Sarah Rapalje, the first white child of European parentage born in the State.' In this, if there is any truth in the depositions of Catalyn or Catalyntie Trico (daughter of Jeremiah Trico of Paris), Sarah's mother, . . . they are clearly mistaken. According to these depositions, she and her husband, Joris Jansen de Rapalje, came to this country in 1623; settled at Fort Orange, now Albany; lived there three years; came, in 1626, to New Amsterdam, 'where she lived afterward for many years; and then came to Long Island, where she now (1688) lives.' Sarah, therefore, was undoubtedly born at Albany, instead of the Walle-boght, and was probably married before she removed to Long Island, there being no reason to suppose that she resided there when a single woman without her husband."

The family record gives the time of her marriage as between her fourteenth and fifteenth year. Mr. Stiles remarks:

"While, therefore, Albany claims the honor of being her birthplace, and New Amsterdam of having seen her childhood, Brooklyn surely received most profit from her; for here in the Wallabout, she was twice married, and gave birth to fourteen children, from whom are descended the Polhemuses, the Bergens, the Bogarts, and many other of the most notable families of Kings County."

At the time of Rapalje's purchase at the Wallabout it began to appear to the land speculators that Long Island was a desirable field. The Director[1] himself made haste to secure the island called "Pagganck," lying close to the Long Island shore south of Fort Amsterdam. The island was thickly covered with nut-trees, which brought it the title of "Nooten" or Nutten Island. In due time this became known as "the Governor's island," and this name has become permanent.

Van Twiller's successor was not less appre-

[1] Van Twiller.

ciative of the value of land on Long Island, but his purchases seem to have been made in the interest of the company. In August, 1638, he bought for the West India Company land adjoining Rapalje's farm and extending between Rennegackonck Creek (at the Wallabout) to Newtown Creek, and inland to " the Swamps of Mespaetches " (Maspeth).

This important sale to Kieft, representing approximately the area of the present Eastern District of Brooklyn, was made by " Kakapoteyuo, Manquenw, and Suwvian, Chiefs of Keskaechquerem," who received " eight fathoms of duffels, eight fathoms of wampum, twelve kettles, eight adzes, and eight axes, with some knives, beads, and awl blades."

By other purchases, at Jersey City and elsewhere, the West India Company sought to extend its dominions and increase the population of the colony. The States-General gave some attention to the colony, and by a proclamation in September, 1638, the Amsterdam Chamber threw open New Netherland to trade by all inhabitants of the United Provinces and of friendly nations, " in the company's ships," with an import duty of fifteen per cent., and an export duty of ten per cent. Every immigrant was to receive from the Director and

Council "according to his condition and means, with as much land as he and his family can properly cultivate," the company reserving a quit-rent of a tenth. To these inducements was added that of free passage over the Atlantic.

The favorable result of these offers soon appeared in the increased rate of immigration and in demand for land. The Director and Council soon found it to be desirable to buy more Long Island land, which they did in January, 1639. By this purchase the company secured the tract extending from Rockaway eastward to "Sicktew-hackey," or Fire Island Bay; thence northward to Martin Gerritsen's, or Cow Bay, and westward along the East River to "Vlaack's Kill"—in other words nearly all the land comprised in the present County of Queens.

In August of the same year (1639) Antony Jansen van Vaas of Saleé received two hundred acres resting within the present towns of New Utrecht and Gravesend. In November a patent was granted for "a tobacco plantation" on the beach, "hard by Saphorakan" (presumably at Gowanus) adjoining the land of Bennett. Another neighbor to Bennett came in the person of Frederick Lubbertsen, who, in May of the following year (1640), received a patent for land extending northerly from Gowanus Cove, and representing a large part of what is now known as South Brooklyn.

Lubbertsen, who had been chief boatswain to Kieft in 1638, was an ambitious and politically disposed man. Two years after this big purchase he was one of twelve men chosen by the commonalty of New Amsterdam. He did not remove to Long Island until 1653, in which year he was chosen to represent the young town of Breuckelen at the New Amsterdam convention. He became a local magistrate in 1653, served several terms thereafter, and filled other political posts.

As the lands of western Long Island represented by the present area of Kings County began to increase in value by increase of settlement and competition in purchase, persons who had merely availed themselves of "squatter" privileges began to see the advisability of taking out formal patents. There had been particularly numerous instances of "squatting" in the region of the Eastern District in a radius from the Wallabout inlet. Among the patents issued in 1640 was one to Abraham Rycken, for a plantation of considerable extent in this region, and in 1641 a piece of

THE FIRST BROOKLYN FERRY

land on the East River legally passed into the possession of Lambert Huybertsen.

Adjoining the land of Joris Rapalje at the Wallabout was an extensive piece of farm land occupied by Rapalje's son-in-law, Hans Hansen Bergen. On Wallabout Bay lay the tobacco plantations of Jan and Peter Montfort, Peter Cæsar, and other farmers. Between the Bay and the East River end of the Lubbertsen purchase came the land sold to Claes Jansen van Naerden (Ruyter), Jan Mauje, and Andries Hudde, all of which was afterward sold to Dirck Janse Waertman, who held it until the sale to his son-in-law, Joris Remsen, in 1706.

Meanwhile (in 1640) the first permanent English settlement on eastern Long Island had been made by Lyon Gardiner on the island which afterward received his name. This settlement, and others which followed it, were distasteful to the West India Company, which, having secured control of the entire western end of the Island, from Cow Bay on the Sound to Canarsie Bay on the ocean side, began to regard itself as entitled to claim jurisdiction over the entire area. When in 1641 emigrants from Lynn, Mass., undertook to settle at Schout's Bay, within Queens County, they were driven off by soldiers who had been sent out by Kieft for the purpose.

The English colonists did not leave the Island, but settled at Southampton, in Suffolk County. The fact that other New England settlers, who planted Southold, were not attacked seems to show either that Kieft scarcely regarded the territory beyond the Queens County line as worth fighting for at this time, or that he came to regard the newcomers as accepting his authority.

The settlement at Southold by emigrants from New Haven was indicative of conditions within New England to which later settlements on Long Island may be attributed. The extreme severity of the Puritan religious temper found expression in distressing exactions and persecutions. Driven from England by intolerance, the Puritans, when placed in control of social and political conditions, exhibited a degree of paternalism not less despotic than that from which they themselves had suffered. And as the Puritans of England had found shelter and liberty in Holland, the victims of Puritanical intolerance in America fled to the friendly support of Dutch authority within the New Netherland jurisdiction.

In fact, shortly after 1640 the Dutch government granted favoring patents to emigrants from New England. The Rev. John Doughty and his followers were welcomed at Maspeth, and provision for other comers (among them Anne Hutchinson and her family) was made at Throg's Neck and New Rochelle.

CHAPTER III

THE INDIANS AND THE EARLY SETTLERS

The Dutch Policy toward the Indians. Puritan and Dutch Policy Contrasted. Long Island Indians: Their Relations with the Whites. Kieft's Attacks on Pavonia and Corlaer's Hook. Uprising on Long Island. Overtures for Peace. Mission to Rockaway of De Vries and Olfertsen. Restoration of Friendly Relations.

THESE numerous settlements had not been accomplished without the encountering of Indian difficulties. In general the Dutch policy toward the Indians was business-like and reasonable, contrasting favorably with policies prevailing elsewhere among American newcomers. The Dutch were not so social as the French, but their attitude was more fraternal than that usually observed among the English colonists. Douglass Campbell, who is to be regarded as a strong partisan of the Dutch as opposed to the Puritan system, but whose exhaustive studies both of the Puritan and of the Dutch people gave him an unusual grasp of the situation, thus contrasts the policy of the two peoples:—

"Why the Puritans were involved in ceaseless wars can be read in every line of their history. As they could not make of the Indian a red Puritan, he was a spiritual outcast, whom it was their duty to exterminate. Three years after the landing of the Mayflower Miles Standish and seven of his companions murdered three native chiefs in cold blood. It was this event which led the devout John Robinson to say, 'How happy a thing it would have been if you had converted some before you killed any.' In 1637 the white settlers of Connecticut put a red captive to death by dragging him limb from limb by ropes fastened to his arms and legs. Bancroft tells us that the Puritans bought the Indians' land, except that of the Pequots. Look at their laws and see. In 1633 Massachusetts passed a statute in relation to land titles. It confirmed to the Indians the little patches around their wigwams on which they raised their corn, but declared that the rest belonged to the whites on the authority of the first chapter of Genesis 'and the invitation of the Indians.' But murder and robbery of their land all pale before the crowning infamy which drove the red man to despair. Above all things he prized personal liberty; slavery to him was a thousand fold worse than death. And yet to this fate the settlers consigned thousands of the natives, sending them to the West Indies to work on the sugar plantations. Among these victims was the little grandson of the good king Massasoit, who had welcomed the Pilgrims and been their life-long friend. Look at the records of Massachusetts, and there you will find statute after statute offering bounties for Indian scalps, the prices fixed being from twenty-five to one hundred pounds for males, from twenty to sixty for women, and from ten to twenty for children under ten years of age. These same statutes provided that females and children taken prisoners should belong to the captors, 'to be sold out of the province.' I mention these facts in no invidious spirit, but in justice to the red man, who has been called treacherous and cruel. He resented such conduct; and can you wonder at it? He had no redress except by arms, and he has written the story of his vengeance all over the face of New England. What could the Indians think of the gospel of Jesus Christ and the white man's God? What was true of the New England colonies was true of the southern colonies as well. The course pursued by Penn can hardly be taken as a criterion, for he dealt with the Delaware Indians, who had been conquered by the Iroquois, deprived of the use of arms, and forced to accept the opprobrious epithet of 'women;' and Penn, in purchasing their lands, only followed out the example which had been set by the Dutch.

"Turn now to New York, and see what the Indian was under different conditions. The upper Hudson and the valley of the Mohawk were first settled by the Dutch. They simply treated the Indian as a man. Tolerant in religion, they respected his rude faith; truthful among themselves, to him they never broke their word; honest in all their dealings with him, they kept good faith. They suffered from no thefts, because they took nothing except by purchase. Their land titles were respected, because for every tract they had an Indian deed. They were scourged by no massacres, save from the enemy across the border, because they committed no robbery or murder. This was the whole secret of their policy. It is easy to belittle it, as historians have done, by saying that upon no other conditions could they have lived among the natives. Of course it was politic, but the world has discovered that honesty is the best policy, without concluding that it is any the less a Christian virtue. These early settlers in New York were traders, offshoots from what was the greatest commercial nation of the world. They made no pretense of doing missionary work. They were simply in pursuit of gain. But they had learned that the only permanent success in life rests on honesty and justice. This is the lesson that commerce teaches, and because it does so it has been the civilizer of the world. After the English conquest in 1664 the same policy was continued, thanks to the presence of the Dutch, who still formed the majority of the population. The Six Nations then placed their lands under protection of the crown and were recognized as appendant to New York. The burden thus cast upon the province was very heavy. For more than a century New York kept their alliance by heavy subsidies and by contributions of men and money for their defense against the French."[1]

The Indian policy of the Dutch has, indeed, been credited with a most important influence upon American history. But sagacious as it may have been as a broad plan of action, there was no way of obviating the difficulties arising from local and individual blunders. Considering the number of special provocations to revolt, it is remarkable that Indian troubles were not more frequent and more serious, and that the storm did not break sooner and more fiercely than it did. Prime remarks that the conduct of the Long Island Indians toward the whites is "without a parallel in the history of the country."

"The Indians on Long Island," says Silas Wood, "seem to have been less troublesome

[1] *Address before Long Island Historical Society*, 1880.

to the whites than those north of the Sound. ... [They] sometimes committed depredations on the property of the whites. ... It does not appear that they ever formed any combination against the first settlers, or materially interrupted the progress of their improvements. ... The security of the whites must be ascribed to the means they employed to preserve peace with the Indians."

When the storm of Indian anger and revenge broke over New England in 1643, New Netherland did not escape a similar if not equally terrible visitation. If the settlers in New Amsterdam began to experience anxiety, something like a panic seized upon the settlers of outlying regions. The Long Island settlers were perhaps less ill at ease than others at an equal distance from the Fort, so friendly had been their relations with the Indians; but individual offenses of the settlers and individual offenses by the Indians produced a strained relation in certain quarters, and when the excuse came the hot-heads among the Long Island settlers made trouble.

At New Amsterdam the trouble began when the Mohawks descended upon the river tribes in retaliation for local offenses, and the river Indians flocked to the vicinity of the Fort for protection. At "Corlaer's Bouwery," on Manhattan Island, a group of Long Island Indians, under the chief, Nainde Nummerius, had encamped. An ill-advised appeal to Kieft resulted in an impulsive decision on the part of the Governor, who, in spite of wiser counsel, sent out two secret expeditions on the night of February 25, 1643, one against the refugees at Pavonia, the other against the encampment at Corlaer's Hook. The attacks were merciless. Eighty Indians were slaughtered at Pavonia, and forty at the Hook.

This unfortunate blunder resulted in acts which still further excited the anger of the Indians. Long Island settlers asked Kieft for permission to attack the Marechawieck tribe; but Kieft, possibly because he had already begun to realize the influence of the outrage he had committed, denied permission on the ground that the Long Island red men had given no sufficient cause for offensive action. Nevertheless, the Governor did not deny to the Long Island settlers any retaliatory steps that might at any time seem necessary. Shortly after this communication, two wagon-loads of corn in charge of a party of Indians were seized, and when the Indians resisted the act of plundering, three of them were killed.

If the massacre on Manhattan Island had caused among the Long Island Indians a general resentment against the white men, the murders on the Island itself made their hostility specific and local; and it is not surprising that many of the Long Island tribes joined hands with the river Indians. The tragedies which followed belong to the annals of a "year of blood."

Terror seized the Long Island settlers in common with all outlying colonists, many of whom lost no time in seeking the shelter of the Fort. Kieft was bewildered by the consequences of his act. Realizing that the chief offenses had been against Long Island tribes, he sent to these a propitiatory message, which was met by shouts of "corn thieves!" by the Indians. Those settlers who held their posts on Long Island were forced to adopt measures of fortifying their homes, which they did after the methods of inclosure peculiar to the time, and to preserve the utmost vigilance to save their lives. From a number of families women and children were sent to the Fort, the men remaining to guard the property.

The advent of spring, bringing to the home-staying Indians of this region, as well as to the white men, the necessity for planting corn, suggested an effort toward permanent peace. Brodhead's narrative says:—

"Three delegates from the wigwam of Penhawity, their 'great chief,' approached Fort Amsterdam, bearing a white flag. 'Who will go to meet them?' demanded Kieft. None were willing but De Vries and Jacob Olfertsen. 'Our chief has sent us,' said the savages, 'to know why you have killed his people, who have never laid a straw in your way, when none has done you aught but good? Come and speak to our chief upon the sea-coast.' Setting out with the Indian messengers, De Vries and Olfertsen, in the evening, came to 'Rechquaaike,' or Rockaway, where they found about three hundred savages and about thirty wigwams. The chief, 'who had but one eye,' invited them to pass the night in his cabin, and regaled them with oysters and fish. At break of day the envoys from Manhattan were conducted into the woods about four hundred yards off, where they found sixteen chiefs of Long Island waiting for their coming. Placing the two Europeans in the centre, the chiefs seated themselves around in a ring, and their 'best speaker' arose, holding in his hand a bundle of small sticks. 'When you first came to our coasts,' slowly began the orator, 'you sometimes had no food; we gave you our beans and corn, and relieved you with our oysters and fish; and now, for recompense, you murder our people;' and he laid down a little stick. 'In the beginning of your voyages, you left your people here with their goods; we traded with them while your ships were away, and cherished them as the apple of our eye; we gave them our daughters for companions, who have borne children, and many Indians have sprung from the Swannekens; and now you villainously massacre your own blood.' The chief laid down another stick; many more remained in his hand; but De Vries, cutting short the reproachful catalogue, invited the chiefs to accompany him to Fort Amsterdam, where the Director 'would give them presents to make a peace.'

"The chiefs, assenting, ended their orations, and presenting De Vries and his colleague each with ten fathoms of wampum, the party set out for their canoes, to shorten the return of the Dutch envoys. While waiting for the tide to rise, an armed Indian, who had been dispatched by a sachem twenty miles off, came running to warn the chiefs against going to Manhattan. 'Are you all crazy, to go to the Fort,' said he, 'where that scoundrel lives who has so often murdered your friends?' But De Vries assured them that 'they would find it otherwise, and come home again with large presents.' One of the chiefs replied at once: 'Upon your words we will go; for the Indians have never heard lies from you, as they have other Swannekens.' Embarking in a large canoe the Dutch envoys, accompanied by eighteen Indian delegates, set out from Rockaway, and reached Fort Amsterdam about three o'clock in the afternoon."

The result of this conference was the reëstablishment of peaceful relations, the Long Island red men aiding in the making of terms with the river Indians. When, in the following September, trouble broke out again, Kieft sought to keep the Long Island tribes as allies, but, before terms could be made, attacks were made at Maspeth and Gravesend, as well as at Westchester; and the ensuing winter was full of distress, most of the settlements becoming almost wholly deserted.

The Government, at its wits' end, appealed to New Haven, and finally to the States-General in Holland itself. In the spring (of 1644) the Long Island Indians were placated; but with the remainder of the hostiles Kieft showed no ability to treat, and the wars lasted until the following year, when the long strain upon Fort Amsterdam was agreeably broken.

CHAPTER IV

THE BEGINNINGS OF BREUCKELEN

1643 – 1647

The Ferry and the Ferry Road. Settlement of Flatlands. Flatbush. Lady Deborah Moody and the Settlement of Gravesend. Early Settlements. The Name of Breuckelen. Henry C. Murphy's Comments. First Schepens and Schout. Commission from the Colonial Council. The Removal of Kieft. Arrival of Stuyvesant.

NEAR the site of the present Peck Slip, New York, there lay, in 1642, a farm owned by Cornelis Dircksen, who kept an inn, and conducted a ferry between a point of land at Peck Slip and a point on the Long Island shore represented by the present location of Fulton Ferry. Dircksen owned land on the Long Island side also, close to the ferry. When he sold this tract in 1643 to William Thomasen, he sold with it the right to run the ferry.

Clustered about the ferry on the Long Island shore were a number of cabins, and the little settlement which grew up there became known in popular parlance as "the Ferry." Crossing the river in the small and rudely built boats of the period was no easy matter, particularly when the tide was in full motion; and the place of crossing was naturally chosen, as at a later time in the building of the great bridge, at the narrowest part.

The irregular road, which wound its way from the ferry on the Long Island side, straggled to the east of the rising ground called by the Indians " Iphetanga," and now known as the Heights, and reached the little settlement of Breuckelen lying at a point closely corresponding to the present City Hall. In fact, the old road followed the general direction of busy Fulton Street of later days.

Before the Indian war of 1643 there were only one or two cabins in this region. To the south lay the first settlement within the limits of Kings County — Amersfoort, or Flatlands. The first recorded purchase of land in this region was by Andries Hudde and Wolphert Gerretsen in 1636. The first plantation here was called Achtervelt, and the house which marked the first settlement is described by Teunis G. Bergen as being twenty-six feet long, twenty-two feet wide, and forty feet high, with a roof " covered above and around with plank; two lofts, one above another, and a small chamber on their side;" while adjoining was "one barn forty feet long, eighteen feet wide, and twenty-four feet deep; and one *bergh* with five posts, forty feet long," the whole surrounded with "long, round palisades."

The road running to Amersfoort turned off at an angle corresponding to the present line of Flatbush Avenue. The road made another turn a short time later, and reached the settlement of Midwout or Flatbush (called by the Dutch *'t Vlaacke Bos*). The actual first settlement of Flatbush, as of the other towns within Kings County, is frequently estimated to have been as early as 1624; but as in the other cases we are obliged to depend for definite knowledge upon records of purchase, which, although they undoubtedly follow, sometimes by a period of several years, the planting of the first habitation, give indication of the time when permanent settlement had begun to be a fact. The town patent from the Director was not secured until 1651.

The ferry road ultimately found its way to the then far town of Jamaica.

Meanwhile, upon that part of Long Island first trodden by the feet of white men had begun the town of Gravesend. The region of Gravesend, including Coney Island (called by the Dutch *'t Conijnen Eylant*) and much of the Bay coast, differed from other regions of the county in being first settled by English people.

Among those who were driven from Connecticut by Puritan intolerance was Lady Deborah Moody. Lady Moody was a daughter of Walter Dunch, a member of the English Parliament in the time of Elizabeth, and widow of Sir Henry Moody of Garsden, in Wiltshire, who had been knighted by King James in 1622. She emigrated to America in 1640, and settled at Swampscott, near Lynn. In her expectation of religious liberty she was disappointed, for the authorities were not long in discovering that she did not regard infant baptism as an ordinance of Divine origin. In those days children a few days old were baptized at church fonts in which the ice had sometimes to be broken before the function could proceed, and the ceremony was regarded as absolutely essential to salvation. Lady Moody was first "admonished," and afterward "presented" to the Quarterly Court for sinfully doubting the wisdom of infant baptism. Excommunicated from the church, and thereby placed in an ostracized position, the distressed English gentlewoman, accompanied by her son, Sir Henry, John Tilton and his wife, and by a few other friends, came to New Amsterdam.[1]

Here she was agreeably surprised to find a few English people who had been living some distance above the Fort, opposite the lower end of Blackwell's Island, but who were at the time of her coming huddled under the walls of the Fort under the terror of the prevailing Indian wars.

A consultation between the Moody party and the Manhattan Island wanderers from New England resulted in the appointment of a committee to select a new site for a settlement. The choice fell upon the Gravesend region, for which Kieft gave a patent in the summer of 1643.

The circumstances under which Gravesend was settled were thus of a promising character, for the party was made up of people who, like Lady Moody, were seeking permanent homes, and were likely to make temperate and energetic citizens. The leader in this band of pioneers was a woman of exceptional force and refinement.

[1] "The Ladye Moodye, a wise and anciently religious woman, being taken with the error of denying baptism to infants, was dealt with by many of the elders and others, and admonished by the church of Salem (whereof she was a member); but persisting still, and to avoid further trouble, etc., she removed to the Dutch against the advice of her friends." — *Governor Winthrop's Journal.*

"For sixteen years," says Stiles, "she went in and out among the people, prominent in their councils, and often intrusted with important public responsibilities, which prove the respect and confidence of her associates. She seems also to have enjoyed the friendship of Governor Stuyvesant, who several times sought her advice in matters of great public importance. Even the nomination of the three town magistrates was, on one or two occasions, intrusted by the Director-General to her good judgment. He also availed himself of her kind offices, on another occasion, in quelling an incipient rebellion, raised by some of her English associates against the Dutch authority."

Whether the name Gravesend was derived from the town of the same name on the Thames, or from the Dutch town Gravensande, is not known, but the stronger reasons are offered for the latter supposition.

Thus, at the close of the Indian wars the meagre settlement of Breuckelen had for company within the area of the present county the hamlets at Flatlands and Gravesend, the farms at the Wallabout, possibly a habitation at Flatbush, and some trading quarters and modest houses at the Ferry. New Utrecht,

Bushwick, Williamsburgh, and New Lots had yet to be settled formally, though squatters, the date of whose coming is impossible to set, began, as soon as the Indian hostilities ceased, to enter upon desirable pieces of land wherever this could be done without local opposition.

The settlement which received the name of Breuckelen was made in the maize region lying between the Wallabout and Gowanus — the latter the place of the first purchase (by Bennett and Bentyn) within the present limits of the city. Portions of this tract were taken by settlers under the Dutch patents from the West India Company. In July, 1645, Jan Evertsen Bout settled here. He was followed a few months later by Huyck Aertsen, Jacob Stoffelsen, Peter Cornielessen, Joris Dircksen, Gerritt Wolfertsen, Cowenhoven, and many others. They located themselves on the road leading from the Ferry to Flatbush, which was then the most important place. A village was formed, which had for its central point the present location of Smith Street and Fulton Avenue.

Henry C. Murphy, writing from Holland at the time of his sojourn as American Minister to that country, describes the Breukelen of Holland as a very old place, containing about

1,500 inhabitants. The houses were old fashioned, and the streets irregular. The people seem to lack thrift and enterprise. The Dutch church was an imposing edifice. Mr. Murphy's impression of the place was not pleasing. Outside of the village he found comfortable dwellings, surrounded with flowers and duck ponds, and everything in perfect neatness and order. On one side of the village was the park, a place laid out with walks and shrubbery, and containing about half an acre of land. He crossed the bridge which spans the Vecht, which connects the two communities, Breukelen Nijenrodes and Breukelen St. Pieters. He speaks of the view as charming. The Vecht is about 100 yards wide, and its waters flow lazily along. "The name Breuckelin," he says, "means marshland." This is the meaning given by the Dutch authorities. Mr. Murphy quotes from one author who says the name has the same origin "as *maarssen*, merely from its marshy and watery turf lands;" and although the name is spelled on ancient documents and letters Bracola, Broecke, Broeckede, Broicklede, and Broeklundia, they all indicate the same origin. Mr. Murphy draws a striking comparison between the character and situation of the two places, showing a wonderful similarity and appropriateness of name, arriving at the conclusion that it was selected on account of the corresponding conditions of the two places. As the Holland Brooklyn was spelled in a variety of ways, so, too, Mr. Murphy says, it has been with our own fair city. He states that the record shows it to have been called Breucklyn, Breuckland, Brucklyn, Brouclyn, Brookland, and Brookline. It was during the close of the last century that its orthography became fixed as Brooklyn.

The circumstances attending the settlement of Breuckelen as a town were associated with a critical turn in the affairs of Kieft's administration.

Kieft's tyrannical methods of government, a form of self-willed procedure absolutely grotesque in many respects, had been sufficiently recognized before the Indian war. After his infamous blunder at Corlaer's Hook his unpopularity increased. Before the war began, Kieft had been compelled to call a Council of Twelve[1] from the people. The Twelve, being chosen by the people, constituted the first illustration offered in New Netherland of representative government. This board, soon

[1] Also described as a Council of Eight.

after the war began, was abolished in a peremptory way; and not long afterward Kieft undertook once more to call upon its advisory aid. When the board objected to certain taxes (on wine, beer, brandy, and beaver skins), he remarked that he still was master, and published his proclamation levying the tax, with the statement that this was done by advice of the council chosen by the commonalty.

To these elected representatives of the people such acts naturally were intolerable, and it was not surprising that they should set themselves to secure the removal of Kieft. A memorial sent to the West India Company asked for his recall and for the introduction of the system of government prevailing in Holland. The College of Nineteen made a report upon the case to the States-General, mentioning incidentally that the colony, started as a commercial enterprise, had cost the West India Company, over all profits, more than 550,000 guilders. The resulting reform considerably modified the theory if not the practice of government in New Netherland. The College of Nineteen decreed a "Supreme Council" for New Netherland. Government was placed in the hands of a council consisting of the Director, a Vice-Director, and a

Fiscal. The people were to have a right to representation in the council, such being desirable "for mutual good understanding, and the common advancement and welfare of the inhabitants."

In the code of general instructions which the West India Company had sent for the guidance of the Provincial Council, those in authority were urged "to do all in their power to induce the colonists to establish themselves in some of the most suitable places, with a certain number of inhabitants, in the manner of towns, villages, and hamlets, as the English are in the habit of doing." It was pursuant to the policy of this code that Bout and his associates declared their intention to "found a town at their own expense."

It fell to the people who were to organize the town of Brooklyn to choose *schepens*;[1] and at this first election they selected as their representatives Jan Evertsen Bout and Huyck Aertsen. Bout was a well-to-do farmer and one of the original settlers. In 1646, he was chosen a schepen to decide questions which might arise in Breuckelen. He took a patent

---

[1] The function of the schepen resembled that of the squire or petty justice, particularly in communities so small as not to have a burgomaster.

from Governor Kieft "of land at Marechkaweick, on the kill of the Gowanus, as well the maize land as the wood land, bounded by the land of Huyck Aertsen." It adjoined the land of Van Cowenhoven, and embraced within its limits the mills which were designated as Frecke's and Denton's. Those mills, situated near each other, are vividly remembered by many Brooklyn citizens. They were reached by a bridge from Butler street. Crossing over the bridge and passing the first mill the road wound around the water's edge.

The commission from the Colonial Council read, as follows: —

"We, William Kieft, Director General, and the Council residing in New Netherland, on behalf of the High and Mighty Lords, States-General of the United Netherlands, His Highness of Orange, and the Honourable Directors of the General Incorporated West India Company. To all those who shall see these presents or hear them read, Greeting : —

"Whereas, Jan Evertsen Bout and Huyck Aertsen, from Rossum, were on the 21st May last unanimously chosen by those interested of Breuckelen, situate on Long Island, as Schepens to decide all questions which may arise, as they shall deem proper, according to the Exemptions of New Netherland granted to Particular Colonies, which election is subscribed by them, with express stipulation that if any one refuse to submit in the premises aforesaid to the above mentioned Jan Evertsen [Bout] and Huyck Aertsen, he shall forfeit the right he claims to land in the allotment of Breuckelen, and in order that everything may be done with more authority, We, the Director and Council aforesaid, have therefore authorized and appointed and do hereby authorize the said Jan Evertsen and Huyck Aertsen to be Schepens of Breuckelen; and in case Jan Evertsen and Huyck Aertsen do hereafter find the labor too onerous, they shall be at liberty to select two more from among the inhabitants of Breuckelen to adjoin them to themselves. We charge and command every inhabitant of Breuckelen to acknowledge and respect the above mentioned Jan Evertsen and Huyck Aertsen as their Schepens, and if any one shall be found to exhibit contumaciousness toward them, he shall forfeit his share as above stated. This done in Council in Fort Amsterdam in New Netherland."

Before the ensuing winter had passed, the schepens found their labors sufficiently arduous to justify an appeal to the Director, which resulted in the appointment of a *schout*, or constable. The new commission said: —

" Having seen the petition of the Schepens

of Breuckelen, that it is impossible for them to tell cases occurring there, especially criminal assaults, impounding of cattle, and other incidents which frequently attend agriculture; and in order to prevent all disorder, it would be necessary to appoint a Schout there, for which office they propose the person of Jan Teunissen. Therefore we grant their request therein, and authorize, as we do hereby authorize, Jan Teunissen to act as Schout, to imprison delinquents by advice of the Schepens, to establish the pound, to impound cattle, to collect fines, and to perform all things that a trusty Schout is bound to perform. Whereupon he has taken his oath at the hands of us and the Fiscal, on whom he shall especially depend, as in Holland substitutes are bound to be dependent on the Upper Schouts or the Bailiff or Marshal. We command and charge all who are included under the jurisdiction of Breuckelen to acknowledge him, Jan Teunissen, for Schout. Thus done in our council in Fort Amsterdam, in New Netherland, the first December, Anno, 1646."[1]

Thus began the official existence of Breuckelen, which at this time was distinct from the hamlets of Gowanus, the Ferry, and the Wallabout. Governor Kieft saw on the Breuck-

---

[1] By the wording of contracts dated November 22, 1646 (New York Col. MSS. ii. 152), it appears that Teunissen was called "Schout of Breuckelen" before this date.

elen shore signs of agricultural activity at various points from Gravesend to beyond the Wallabout. In March, 1647, Hans Hansen Bergen bought a large tract of land adjoining the farm of his father-in-law, Joris Jansen de Rapalje. The water frontage of this tract was from the Wallabout Creek to the line of the present Division Avenue. Other purchases on the shore probably completed the chain of private ownership along the river and bay fronts between the points above named. A second tier of patents represented land back of the river parcels, and sometimes running in very eccentric lines.

Although these patents antedated in many instances by several years the actual settlement by the owners,[1] the increasing number gave indication of the stimulus that came with the end of organized Indian hostilities. The cessation of these hostilities brought new life to the people of New Netherland, and induced them to look more critically at the urgencies of their political as well as their domestic situation.

The movement looking to the removal of

---

[1] As we have seen, Rapalje, who made one of the earliest purchases (1636), did not begin living on his Wallabout farm until probably 1655.

Kieft, which first resulted in modifications in the form of government, and which had never slumbered, at last succeeded, and in May, 1647, Kieft was succeeded by Peter Stuyvesant.

CHAPTER V

DOMESTIC AND SOCIAL LIFE UNDER THE DUTCH

1647–1664

Beginning of Stuyvesant's Administration. Condition of the Colony. Character of the Early Dutch Houses. Household Arrangement. Dress. Funerals. Marriages. The Mixture of Races. Slavery. Religion. Attitude of Stuyvesant toward Sects other than Dutch Reformed. Triumph of Liberal Ideas. First Churches in Kings County. Troubles over the Church Tax. First Schools. The Dutch and Popular Education. End of Dutch Rule.

WHEN Stuyvesant, followed by the principal burghers, made his first public appearance in New Amsterdam, the people saw that the new Director had but one leg, the other, which he had lost in the wars, having been replaced by a wooden affair, laced with silver bands. His manner was soldierly, and excited from those who looked askance at him the remark that his stride was "like a peacock's, with great pomp and state." Moreover he was accused of keeping the burghers bareheaded for several hours, though he was covered, "as if he were the Czar of Muscovy."

Peter Stuyvesant[1] was the son of a clergyman of the Reformed Church. He was a "self-made" man, having had a hard struggle from his boyhood. He had fought in the service of the West India Company against the Spaniards and Portuguese in South America. For a time he was Governor of the Island of Curaçoa, and it was while making an attack, during this command, on the Island of St. Thomas that he lost his leg. He had married, at Amsterdam, Judith, the daughter of Balthazzar Bayard, a French Protestant who, like so many others who came to America, had fled to Holland to escape persecution.

When Stuyvesant declared in his first speech at the Fort that he would govern the colony "as a father does his children," he gave some hint of the view of the situation which he was inclined to take. However fatherly and generous were his feelings toward the people whom he was to preside over, he intended to be master of the situation.

The people who greeted the new Director

[1] "No other figure of Dutch, nor indeed of Colonial days is so well remembered; none other has left so deep an impress on Manhattan history and tradition as this whimsical and obstinate, but brave and gallant old fellow, the kindly tyrant of the little colony. To this day he stands in a certain sense as the typical father of the city." — Theodore Roosevelt, *New York*, p. 26.

with much cordiality, and who in this demonstration were influenced as greatly by the feeling that any change must be for the better as by any definite expectation that Stuyvesant would be better than Kieft, had suffered from so many influences that tended to disorganize and disconcert them that the new Director found them in no very promising state. Indeed, he found New Netherland in a "low condition."

Breuckelen and her sister settlements were as yet merely farming communities. New Amsterdam itself had begun to present some of the characteristics of a town. Extending as far as the present line of Wall Street (from which fact the street gets its name), it was thickly settled within a narrow area toward the point. The houses were rough, the streets unkempt. "Pig-pens and out-houses were set directly on the street, diffusing unpleasant odors. The hogs ran at will, kept out of the vegetable gardens only by rough stockades."[1]

If the physical condition of the town offended Stuyvesant, so, also, did the moral condition. The new Director called for a "thorough reformation." There must be an end of drunkenness, Sabbath-breaking, and the selling of

[1] Bayard Tuckerman, *Peter Stuyvesant*, p. 62.

liquors to the Indians. Stuyvesant saw the necessity of conciliating the Indians, and the efforts which he made to this end were gratifying to the Long Island settlers.

To protect the outlying settlements from the incursions of the savages, and to provide means for the payment of the annual presents and perquisites to the Indians, Stuyvesant consented to give the various towns representation in the government. The grand old democratic principle of taxation and representation going hand in hand was thus recognized. It was these sentiments, which early took root in Breuckelen, that resulted in the Revolutionary War, and established the fact that taxation without representation was unjustifiable. As a result of this consent, an election was held in Breuckelen and the other towns, and eighteen of the most respectable and honored men in the community were chosen, from whom nine were selected by the Director and Council as an advisory board. They were to confer with the Director and Council and to promote the welfare of the people. They were also to consult upon all measures proposed by the Director and Council, and to give their advice. The Director was empowered to preside at all meetings of this board. The members held seats in the Council, taking turns weekly, three sitting at a time; on court days acting in a judicial capacity to try cases and render judgment.

The administration, at least in its earlier years, saw an increase in the rate of immigration. During Stuyvesant's administration many stone houses appeared in New Amsterdam, and on Long Island came an improved class of habitations.

The houses of the Dutch period, and of the later period that imitated the primitive architecture of that time, are among the most interesting objects of study that remain on Long Island. The first Long Island houses had resembled those of the Indians. Very soon afterward the character of the dwellings became more solid and permanent, and after the Indian war came comfortable one-story houses, thatched with straw, and with big stone chimneys. Most of the Dutch houses on Long Island, even in later times, were of wood. A brickyard was established at New Amsterdam in 1660; but in those days it was thought that the baking of brick of greater thickness than two inches could not be effectual, and building with such small brick as then came from the maker was very expensive.

The one-story Dutch houses generally had an "overshoot" roof, which formed now one and now two piazzas. Very often a seat was placed at each end of the porch; and when the weather permitted, this sheltered place was generally occupied by the family and visitors of an evening. There are a number of these fine old Dutch houses still standing within the limits of the county and city.

The interior of the Dutch houses was generally as solid and simple as the exterior. The big fireplace was one of the most important features of the house. Those who could afford it often had the mantel front set about with glazed Holland tiles. These tiles had pictures moulded on them, and very often the whole series of pictures around the fireplace opening would tell stories from the Bible. "The children grew to know these pictures, and the stories they told, by heart; and when they gathered about the hearth of an evening, and the tile pictures glimmered faintly in the light of the big wood fire, grandfather would open the great family Bible on his knees and read some of the stories over again for the hundredth time."

In the best room of the house stood the mountainous bedstead, as grand as the owner could afford to make it. Underneath was the trundle-bed, which was pulled out at night for the children to sleep on.

"The pillow-cases were generally of check patterns; and the curtains and valance were of as expensive materials as their owner could afford; while in front of the bed a rug was laid, for carpets were not then in common use. Among the Dutch the only article of that sort, even up to the time of the Revolution, was a drugget of cloth, which was spread under the table during meal-time when, upon 'extra occasions,' the table was set in the parlor. But even these were unknown among the inhabitants of Breuckelen and the neighboring towns. The uniform practice, after scrubbing the floor well on certain days, was to place upon the damp boards the fine white beach sand (of which every family kept a supply on hand, renewing it by trips to the seashore twice a year), arranged in small heaps, which the members of the family were careful not to disturb by treading upon; and on the following day, when it had become dry, it was swept, by the light and skillful touch of the housewife's broom, into waves or other more fanciful figures. Rag carpets did not make their appearance in this country until about the beginning of the present century."[1]

[1] Stiles, *History of Brooklyn*, vol. i. p. 229.

The Dutch did not use tables save for the kitchen or for the service of meals. The table dishes were of wood and pewter, though a few people kept some china on the sideboard for "company." As tea was a luxury which very few had much of, the tea cups were very small. For display, silver tankards, beakers, porringers, spoons, snuffers, and candlesticks were in favor. Clocks were extremely rare, the primitive hour-glass doing service in most houses. "Of books," says Stiles, "our ancestors had but few, and these were mostly Bibles, Testaments, and Psalm-Books. The former, many of which still exist among the old families, were quaint specimens of early Dutch printing, with thick covers, and massive brass, and sometimes silver, corner-pieces and clasps. The Psalm-Books were also adorned with silver edgings and clasps, and, when hung by chains of the same material to the girdle of matrons and maidens fair, were undoubtedly valued by their owners quite as much for the display which they made as for their intrinsic value."

In every family was a spinning-wheel,— sometimes four or five. The dress of the people, like so many other Dutch things, closely resembled that of Hollanders at home. The ordinary dress for men was a blouse or jacket, and wide, baggy trousers. Justices and other officials wore black gowns. The Sunday clothes of men as well as women were often gorgeous in color and effect. The ladies frizzed and powdered their hair, wore silk hoods in place of hats, and squeezed their feet into very high-heeled shoes. The dandies of the day wore long coats with silver lace and silver buttons, bright vests or waistcoats, velvet knee-breeches, black silk stockings, and low shoes with silver buckles.

On holidays the people made a gay-looking company. Christmas was a happy festival with them always. In those early days people had to depend upon such family festivities even more than do later generations having many sources of amusement away from home. It was from the Dutch that American children learned to say Santa Claus, and it was from them that Americans learned that fashion, which has still not entirely died out, of making calls on New Year's Day.

One of the prudent customs of the Dutch settlers was to begin, so soon as they came of age, to lay by money for their funeral expenses. No Dutchman wanted to be a burden upon any one if he could help it, even when he died, and this practice of laying by gold or silver pieces to pay the expenses of proper burial became very general. A Dutch funeral was one of the most singular features of life among the people. After the minister had seated himself beside the coffin and the company was duly assembled, the sexton or servants would appear with glasses and decanters, and wine would be given to such of the guests as cared to drink. Funeral cakes and other victuals were handed about in the same way, and then pipes and tobacco were brought in. The eating, drinking, and smoking being finished, the minister would rise and make his address and prayer, and then the sexton and minister would lead the procession to the burying-ground.[1]

[1] "Among the Dutch settlers the art of stone-cutting does not appear to have been used until within comparatively a few years, with but few exceptions, and their old burying-grounds are strewn with rough head-stones which bear no inscriptions; whereas the English people, immediately on their settlement, introduced the practice of perpetuating the memories of their friends by inscribed stones. Another reason for not finding any very old tombstones in the Dutch settlements is that they early adopted the practice of having family burying-places on their farms, without monuments, and not unfrequently private burials, both of which the Governor and Colonial Legislature, in 1664 and 1684, deemed of sufficient importance to merit legislative interference, and declared that all persons should be publicly buried in some parish burial-place." — Furman, *Antiquities of Long Island*, p. 155.

A people so prudent about matters of funeral expenses were likely to be prudent about other affairs of life coming earlier in the list. Young men were generally careful about saving money with which to get married, and the young women spun and sewed for many months getting ready the linen which they were in the habit of providing for the housekeeping.

Furman instances this inventory of the goods a Breuckelen bride brought to her husband: "A half-worn bed, two cushions of ticking with feathers, one rug, four sheets, four cushion covers, two iron pots, three pewter dishes, one pewter basin, one iron roaster, one schuyrn spoon, two cowes about five years old, one case or cupboard, one table."

That the course of true love, as it is observed after marriage, did not always run smooth, is shown by the early appointment in New Amsterdam of a "First Commissary of Marriage Affairs."

In this era marriage was surrounded with many difficulties, and required both time and patience to secure its accomplishment. The following curious document is the form which was used in 1654 to secure a marriage license: —

To the right Honourable the Lordships the Magistrates of Gravesend:

DEAR FRIENDS — Whereas, on the date of this 10th day of February, 1654, a peticion is presented to the cort hereby, Johannes Van Beeck, that the banns (of matrimonie) between him and Maria Varleth, may bee hear registered and bee properly proclaimed, and wee hav understoode that the same Johannes Van Beeck ande Maria Varleth had prevusly too this maide procklemation of thare banns throgh youre cort att Gravesende wich (under Koncison) is contrarie too the stile and customes of oure Faderland. Itt is oure requeste to youre honourable cort in case such an ockacion should ockur in futur, that wee mai bee inn formed kincerneing the same, inn order on ether sydde to preventee all impropriertys, which allso wee engaige too doo on our parte spechally iz the praktize and custome off our Faderland that any one shal maike three procklamations inn the plaice ware his domercile is, ande then he maye bee maryed werever hee pleases, wherein wee ar ande remain your right Honourable Lordships' affectionate friend.

ARENT VAN HATTAN.

Bye order of thee Burgomasters and Shepens of New Amsterdam. Attest

JACOB KIPP, Sec'ty.

AMSTERDAM IN NIEW NETHERLANDS, this 10th day of February, 1654.

The next step taken by the candidates for matrimony was their appearance before the Court. This event in the old manuscripts is recorded as follows: —

"Casper Varleth and Johannes Van Beeck appeared inn cort and praed most ernestly thatt onn thee perticion and remonstrance konserning the marriage between Johannes Van Beeck and Maria Varleth presented too the Burgomasters and Schepens may be disposed off, and in konsequence of the Bench note being kompleate itt iz posponed untill Thursda next, soe az inn thee meantime too notifie the other Lordships.

"Johannes Van Beeck appeared in cort and requested az before thatt acion maye bee had onn his peticion, offering furthermore iff thort nesary att thee time ande the okeacion too bee readie to affirme under oathe whatt he stated inn his peticion, repeating especially three conversacions hadd with his Excellencie Petrus Stuyvesant."

The subject-matter of the petition was important, and could not be hastily passed upon. The Burgomasters deliberated for three days, and doubtless viewed the subject in every phase and light imaginable. At last they reached a conclusion which cannot be better presented than in the precise language of the decision rendered: —

"Bye the Burgomasters and Shepens of niew amsterdam — having been seen and examined the peticion as presentede too our cort, onn the 10th ande 16th days of this month, tochinge the bonds off matrimonie between Joh Van Beeck and Maria Varleth. Tharefore wee inquire into,

"First — Who frome the beginning was the institutor of marriage, ande also whot the apostels off thee Gentiles teaches thareon.

"Secondly — The proper and attaned age of Johannes Van Beeck ande Maria Varleth.

"Thirdlie — Thee consente off the Fathure ande Mothure off the Dauter.

"Forthly — The distance and remoutnes beetweene this and oure Faderland, together withe thee calamiters relacion betweene Holland and England.

"Fifthly — Thee danegur in such case arisienge ffrom long retardacion, betweene these too younge persons beecominge publick blame being attachede to the fammelys onn either sidde.

"Our Shurlogans ande wise Jurists doo saye korectly onn such mattus, that wee must nott commit any lesser sinns too avoyde grater ones; therefore wee thinke (with due submission) thatt bye suteable marrage (the apostel inn his epistel to the Heebrues calls the bedd undefiled honurable) both thee lesser ande thee grater crimes are preevented. Tharefor thee Burgomasters and Shepens off the city of Niew Amsterdam doe judge thatt thee afforeseyde younge persons haveing mayde thare proper Ecklisiastical proclamations with the earlyst opportunitie, and that they folloe it upp with thee bonds of matrimonie immediatelie tharafter.

"Done at the Stadt House inn Niew Amsterdam in Niew Netherlands this 19th Feberary, 1654.

"ARENT VAN HATTAN, MARTIN KRIGIER,
P. L. VANDUGRIST, WILH. BEECKMAN,
PIETER WOLFERSON, JOSH. P. R. RUYTER,
OLOFF STEVENSEN."

The social life of the New Netherlands was in many respects characteristic of the hard conditions of life in any new country, but in many respects it was peculiarly different from that of New England. "The sharp and strong contrasts in social position," says Mr. Roosevelt,[1] "the great differences in moral and material well-being, and the variety in race, language, and religion, all combined to make a deep chasm between life in New Amsterdam and life in the cities of New England, with their orderly uniformity of condition and their theocratic democracy." In fact, democratic as the Dutch theory was, the actual condition of

[1] *New York*, p. 29.

the Dutch colony was aristocratic in its characteristics. "The highest rank was composed of the great patroons, with their feudal privileges and vast landed estates; next in order came the well-to-do merchant burghers of the town, whose ships went to Europe and Africa, carrying in their holds now furs or rum, now ivory or slaves; then came the great bulk of the population, — thrifty souls of small means, who worked hard, and strove more or less successfully to live up to the law; while last of all came the shifting and intermingled strata of the evil and the weak, — the men of incurably immoral propensities, and the poor whose poverty was chronic."

The picturesqueness of the population was accentuated by the presence of a growing number of negro slaves which a Dutch vessel had been the first to bring to America.[1] But, as we shall see later, slavery never was welcomed as an institution in this region, and never gained a firm foothold. Tobacco culture and other causes, which operated to the encouragement of slavery in Virginia and Maryland, did not appear in the northern colonies; where, moreover, the temper and taste of the people

---

[1] A Dutch war-ship sold twenty negroes into the colony of Virginia in August, 1619.

were not such as to make easy the development of slavery.

As in early New England, the domestic and social affairs of the Dutch colony were always intimately associated with religious traditions, and, as in New England, the theory of religious liberty found a varying and often a grotesque application.

The early theory of the colony was that of complete religious liberty, and at no time was there an intolerance comparable to that which prevailed among the Puritans, who sought liberty but yielded little; but the laws of the colony favored the Protestant Reformed Church, and it alone. To be sure, the West India Company commended freedom of belief, and the early Governors, partly, doubtless, because they were too busy with other matters, and partly because occasion had not yet arisen, caused little trouble by any attitude toward questions of faith or worship. But when the colony grew to considerable proportions, and the mixture of races brought about by the advertised liberality of the Dutch settlements began to bring up the social and religious questions inevitable in such a community, there were many clashings and disputes and bitternesses.

Stuyvesant was as definite and immovable in his ideas about church-going as about everything else. He believed in established authority, and personally resented the impertinence of people who saw fit to take a position at variance with what seemed to be set forth and settled by the established power. When the Lutherans, in 1654, sought to hold meetings of their own, Stuyvesant reminded them of the duty of attending the good Dutch church, and refused them premises for their meetings.

Appeal to Holland, whose position Stuyvesant's mental methods certainly did not represent in this instance, forced the Director to let the Lutherans alone; and possibly the rebuke was responsible for the fact that the Anabaptists on Long Island escaped serious trouble shortly afterward. But Stuyvesant hated the "cursed Quakers," with whom he had many bitter differences, going so far as to hang up one preacher by the arms and lash him for defying his authority.

Of Catholics Stuyvesant had an even greater horror. In 1654, he passed an ordinance forbidding the keeping of Ash Wednesday and all other holy days, as "heathenish and popish institutions, and as dangerous to the public peace."

To the intermittent religious squabbles brought on by the determination of Stuyvesant to stick to the letter of the law rather than to take the popular Dutch view of moderate leniency, the West India Company finally put a stop by ordering Stuyvesant to "let every one remain free so long as he is modest, moderate, his political conduct irreproachable, and as long as he does not offend others or oppose the Government." These terms, rather than any ever offered by Stuyvesant, represent the real sentiment prevalent among the Dutch people.

In the ship which brought over Governor Minuit, in 1626, came two *ziekentroosters*, or "comforters of the sick," who were frequently found filling positions as assistants to ordained clergymen. By these two men the early religious services of the New Amsterdam colony were conducted until 1628, when another ship from Holland brought out Jonas Michaelius, who was sent by the North Synod of the Netherlands. It was Michaelius who "first established the form of a church" at Manhattan. He was succeeded five years later by Everardus Bogardus, whose congregation left the upper loft of the horse-mill for a small building dedicated to church service. In

1642, a new stone church was built within the Fort, and in the year of Stuyvesant's coming Bogardus was succeeded by Dominie Johannes Megapolensis, who led the church for twenty-two years.

Meanwhile the Long Island settlers who wished to attend divine service were obliged to cross the river to New Amsterdam. In 1654, however, Midwout (Flatbush), which had begun to assume an importance as a settlement that promised to give it the position that Breuckelen afterward assumed, established a church. An order was issued in February, 1655, requiring the inhabitants of Breuckelen and Amersfoort (Flatlands) to assist Midwout "in cutting and hauling wood" for the church. The Breuckelen people objected to working on the minister's house, but were forced, under the Governor's order, to assist throughout the work.

This first church in Kings County, built under the supervision of Dominie Megapolensis, John Snedicor, and John Stryker, occupied several years in the building; but that it was used before its completion is indicated by the fact that in August, 1655, Stuyvesant convened the inhabitants to give their opinion as to the qualifications of the Rev. Johannes Theodorus

Polhemus as a "provisional minister," and to decide what salary they would pay him. The report of the Schout was that the people approved of Mr. Polhemus, and that they would pay him 1,040 guilders (about $416) a year.

Polhemus belonged to "an ancient and highly respectable family" in the Netherlands, had been a missionary in Brazil, and had come from that country to New Amsterdam. He was a devout Christian, and his faithfulness does not seem to have been questioned, but when, in 1656, the magistracy of Midwout and Amersfoort sought permission to request voluntary contributions from the three Dutch towns, Breuckelen protested, declaring that "as the Rev. John Polhemus only acts as a minister of the Gospel in the village of Midwout, therefore the inhabitants of the village of Breuckelen and adjacent districts are disinclined to subscribe or promise anything for the maintenance of a Gospel minister who is of no use to them." By way of showing their good will to Mr. Polhemus personally, they urged that the minister might be permitted to preach alternately in Breuckelen and Midwout. If this were done they were " very willing to contribute cheerfully to his support, agreeable to their abilities."

The Director and Council replied that they had "no objection that the Reverend Polhemus, when the weather permits, shall preach alternately in both places;" but although Midwout consented, Gravesend and Amersfoort objected, these villages having contributed to the support of the Midwout church, and Breuckelen being "quite two hours' walking from Amersfoort and Gravesend, whereas the village of Midwout is not half so far and the road much better." To this was added: "So they considered it a hardship to choose either to hear the gospel but once a day, or to be compelled to travel four hours, in going and returning, all for one single sermon, which would be to some very troublesome, and to some utterly impossible."

As a way out of this difficulty the Director and Council decided that the morning sermon should be at Midwout, which was about the same distance from each of the three other towns, and that the afternoon service should be changed to an evening service to be held alternately in Breuckelen and Amersfoort. In recognition of the situation of Midwout, that village was to give annually 400 guilders, and Breuckelen and Amersfoort each 300 guilders for the support of the minister.

This seemed like an amicable settlement, and might have remained such had not Breuckelen been dissatisfied with the preaching of Mr. Polhemus. The dissatisfaction expressed itself in a protest sent to the Director and Council, in which the people of Breuckelen reminded the Director that they had never called the Reverend Polhemus, and had never accepted him as their minister. "He intruded himself upon us against our will," said the protest, "and voluntarily preached in the open street, under the blue sky; when to avoid offense, the house of Joris Dircksen was temporarily offered him." Moreover, Mr. Polhemus was accused of offering "a poor and meagre service," giving, every fortnight, "a prayer in lieu of a sermon," by which they could receive "very little instruction." Often, when they supposed this prayer was beginning, it was "actually at an end." This they experienced on the Sunday preceding Christmas, when, expecting an appropriate sermon, they heard "nothing but a prayer." "Wherefore," continues the protest, "it is our opinion that we shall enjoy as much and more edification by appointing one among ourselves, who may read to us on Sundays, a sermon from the 'Apostles' Book,' as we ever have until now from any of the prayers or sermons of the Reverend Polhemus." All this, the protest hastened to say, was intended in no offense to the preacher, whose inabilities were recognized as resulting naturally from the fact that in his advanced years "his talents did not accompany him as steadily as in the days of yore."

To this protest Stuyvesant responded merely by directing the sheriff to "remind those of Breuckelen, once more, to fulfil their engagement, and to execute their promise relative to the salary of Mr. Polhemus." Amid their discontent, and in consequence also of the poverty of many of his parishioners, the poor preacher suffered not a little for want of the ordinary necessities of life. In the winter of 1656, his house being not yet completed, he and wife and children were forced to sleep on the floor. When Sheriff Tonneman complained to the Council of having been abused while attempting to collect the odious tax, Lodewyck Jong, Jan Martyn, "Nicholas the Frenchman, Abraham Janesen the mulatto, and Gerrit the wheelwright," were each fined twelve guilders ($4.80); and when Jan Martyn sought to hire the public bellman to defame Tonneman, he was "obliged to beg pardon, on bended knees, of the Lord and of the court, and was fined twenty-five guilders ($10) and costs."

Wearied of his efforts to coax and threaten the Breuckelen opposition into paying the tax, Stuyvesant at last (in July, 1658) forbade all inhabitants of the three towns to remove grain from their fields until all tithes were taken or commuted. There was no escape from this, and the tax was paid.

Two years later Breuckelen secured a preacher of her own in the person of the Rev. Henricus Selyns,[1] a preacher whose ancestors had been prominent in the earliest days of the Dutch Reformed Church, and who had been reared in the traditions of this flourishing denomination. He engaged to serve Breuckelen for four years.

When, in September, 1660, Dominie Selyns preached his first sermon in the Breuckelen barn which served as a house of worship, the population of the village was one hundred and thirty-four persons, representing thirty-one families. The preacher had been promised a salary of one hundred florins, but when an effort was made to raise funds the magistrates

---

[1] The call of the Breuckelen Church to Dominie Selyns was by him accepted, and approved by the Classis of Amsterdam, February 16, 1660(-61). — *Brooklyn Church Records.*

found themselves under the necessity of appealing to the Director for aid. Stuyvesant offered to pay one hundred and fifty guilders, provided Mr. Selyns would also preach every afternoon at his "bouwery" on Manhattan Island. This arrangement was duly made. In 1661, when Breuckelen received from the West India Company, by request of Dominie Selyns, a bell for the church, there were fifty-two communicants. Meanwhile, Mr. Selyns was living at New Amsterdam, and in 1662 an effort was made to induce the preacher to live in Breuckelen, on the theory of the schepens that, if he did so bring himself among them, "the community would be more willing and ready to bring in their respective quotas." It does not appear that the Dominie found it convenient to live in Breuckelen, but there is no doubt of his zeal nor of his popularity. When, in 1664, the Dominie returned to Holland, it was with the regrets and good wishes of the little band of Breuckelen parishioners.

The Dutch attitude toward education was in many respects very different from that which prevailed among the English. At the time of the settlement of New England and New Amsterdam, Holland was far in advance of other European states in ideas of popular education. Mr. Campbell[1] places Holland two hundred years in advance of any other country in Europe at the time of the Puritan emigration. There was, indeed, an extraordinary contrast between "the free cities" of the Netherlands and their neighbors at this time. "The whole population," says May,[2] "was educated. The higher classes were singularly accomplished. The University of Leyden was founded for the learned education of the rich, and free schools were established for the general education." Common schools had, indeed, been founded in the sixteenth century, and in the seventeenth the children of all classes were taught at the public expense.

Such ideas of educational democracy had

[1] Mr. Campbell and other recent writers, actuated doubtless by some resentment toward the complacency of New England, have unquestionably exaggerated in certain respects the essential position of Holland in educational advancement, and offered a somewhat stronger plea for the leadership of the Dutch in popular education on this continent than a strictly judicial examination of the case seems to justify; but there can be no reasonable doubt in the minds of impartial students that serious misconceptions have existed, and that these justify the championship of the Dutch, of which Mr. Campbell's *The Puritan in Holland, England, and America* is so brilliant an example. The early claims for English and for Puritan educational traditions not only ignored but excluded the Dutch, and it was inevitable that the effort to do justice to Holland's remarkable services for popular education should result in occasional overstatement.

[2] *Democracy in Europe*, vol. ii. pp. 67-72.

not appeared in England at the time when education first began to be considered in this country. Mr. Draper[1] notes that there was no school but the Latin school in Boston for thirty-five years after the passage of the so-called compulsory education law of 1647. Nor did the early Massachusetts schools receive all the children of the people. "No boys were received under seven years of age till 1818. No girls of any age were admitted prior to 1789. It was one hundred and forty-two years after the passage of the so-called compulsory school law of 1647 before Boston admitted one girl to her so-called 'free schools,' and it was one hundred and eighty-one years thereafter before girls had facilities equal to those enjoyed by their brothers."

On the other hand, New Amsterdam had a professional schoolmaster as early as 1633, and with him popular common school education began in this country. Prior to 1662, there were as many as ten persons licensed to keep private schools or to teach on their own account, and Furman states that young men from both the New England and the Virginia colonies came to New Amsterdam to be edu-

[1] *Public School Pioneering in New York and Massachusetts.*

cated. Speaking of the movement of 1658, looking to the establishment of a Latin school at New Amsterdam, and of the comment thereon by Mr. George H. Martin, representing the State Board of Education of Massachusetts, Mr. Draper says: —

"Mr. Martin seems to make much of the fact that the petition for the sending over of a Latin master stated that there was no Latin school nearer than Boston, but overlooks the fact that there had previously been a Latin school at New Amsterdam, and also the other fact that there was no school at Plymouth, and none but a Latin school at Boston, and that it received only a few of the brighter boys of the wealthier families, to prepare them for college and the ministry."

The earliest laws of the colony show that for the support of schools "each householder and inhabitant should bear such tax and public charge as should be considered proper for their maintenance."[1]

The first schoolmaster in Breuckelen made his appearance in 1661, on the 4th day of July, in which year the following petition was presented: —

[1] *New York Colonial Documents*, vol. i. p. 112.

To the Right Hon. Director-General and Council of New Netherland:—

The Schout and Schepens of the Court of Breuckelin respectfully represent: That they found it necessary, that a court messenger was required for the Schepens Chamber, to be occasionally employed in the Village of Breuckelin, and all around, where he may be needed, as well to serve summons, as also to conduct the service of the church, and to sing on Sunday; to take charge of the school, dig graves, etc.; ring the bell and perform what ever else may be required. Therefore, the petitioners, with your Honours' approbation, have thought proper to accept for so highly necessary office a suitable person who is now come before them, one Carel Van Beauvois, to whom they have appropriated the sum of fl. 150, beside a fine dwelling; and whereas the petitioners are apprehensive that the aforesaid C. V. Beauvois would not and cannot do the work for the sum aforesaid, and the petitioners are not able to promise him any more; therefore the petitioners, with all humble and proper reverence, request your Honours to be pleased to lend them a helping hand, in order thus to receive the needful assistance. Herewith awaiting your Honours' kind and favorable answer, and commending ourselves, Honorable, wise, prudent and most discreet gentlemen, to your favor, we pray for your Honours God's protection, together with a happy and prosperous administration, unto salvation. Your Honors' servants and subjects, the Schout and Schepens of the village aforesaid. By order of the same,

[Signed]   ADRIAEN HEGEMAN, Secretary.

The Directors granted the petition and agreed to pay fifty guilders annually in wampum for the support of the precentor and schoolmaster.

The first school was set up in the little church, which stood near the present junction of Fulton and Bridge Streets. The second public school within the county was opened in the new village of Bushwick.

The area of the county represented by the town of Bushwick had, as we have seen, been purchased by the West India Company in 1638. In 1660 the Wallabout residents had built a block-house on the high point of land overlooking the East River, known as the "Kiekout,"[1] or "Lookout." At about the same time (in the month of February), "fourteen Frenchmen, with a Dutchman named

---

[1] The river farm, which included the "Kiekout" bluff, is first found in the possession of Jean Meserole, who came from Picardy, France, in 1663, and from whom is descended Gen. Jeremiah V. Meserole, President of the Williamsburgh Savings Bank, first colonel of the Forty-seventh Regiment, N. G. S. N. Y.

Peter Janse Wit" and an interpreter, called upon the Director to lay out a town plot east of the Wallabout settlement. On February 19 the Director, with the Fiscal, Nicasius de Sille, Secretary Van Ruyven, and the sworn surveyor, Jaques Corteleau, came to a spot between "Mispat (Maspeth) Kill," Newtown Creek, and "Norman's Kill,"[1] Bushwick Creek, to "establish a village." Here a survey was made, and twenty house lots laid out. The first house was at once erected by Evert Hedeman, and others soon appeared.

In March of the following year "the Director-General visited the new village, when the inhabitants requested His Honour to give the place a name; whereupon he named the town Boswijck," the Town of the Woods. The people of the new village then selected six of their men, from which the governor chose three, to be magistrates, the town remaining subject to the schout of Breuckelen, Amersfoort, and Midwout.

Thus when the first public school was

[1] So named from Dirck Volckertsen, surnamed "the Norman," to whom was granted in 1645 land on the East River between Bushwick Creek and Newtown Creek, now within the seventeenth ward of the city of Brooklyn, and still known as Greenpoint. Volckertsen lived in a stone house on the northerly side of Bushwick Creek near the East River. The house was standing until after the middle of the present century.

opened in Bushwick, the hamlet scarcely contained twenty houses, a fact which may illustrate the attitude of the Dutch and French in this part of the country toward the question of popular education. The first schoolmaster in Bushwick was Boudwyn Manout, who took charge on December 28, 1662.

The setting up of the third school within the county was effected in a new village called Bedford, lying southeast of the Wallabout and east of Breuckelen. The settlement of this village dates from 1662, in which year, in the month of March, Joris Jan. Rapalje, Teunis Gysbert (Bogaert), Cornelis Jacobsen, Hendrick Sweers, Michael Hans (Bergen), and Jan Hans (Bergen) asked the Director for a grant of unoccupied woodland " situated in the rear of Joris Rapalje, next to the old Bay Road." The Director made the grant, with the stipulation that the petitioners should not make " a new hamlet."

The little settlement thus formed was adjacent on the south to another known as Cripplebush[1] (variously spelt in the Dutch orthography of the early days), and lay at the

[1] Early section names within the township of Breuckelen were Gowanus, Red Hook (lying west of the Ferry), the Ferry, Wallabout, Bedford, Cripplebush. All of these, save the last, have survived as designations of regions in the present city.

intersection of the Jamaica highway, the Clove Road running to Flatbush, and the Cripplebush Road running to Newtown.

The Bedford school-house was placed in the heart of the village, at the cross-roads. This school, beginning in the year 1663, afterward, according to the records of Teunis G. Bergen, became the present Public School No. 3, and had an interesting history.

Throughout the whole of Stuyvesant's directorship, the quarrels between him and the people were of frequent occurrence, and gained rather than diminished in violence. As we have seen, the tendency observable in the colony was aristocratic, and Stuyvesant fostered such a tendency to the utmost. At one time he sought to institute a division of the burghers into two classes, major and minor, the rights of the major burghers to be hereditary, and to include the sole right to hold office. He had an honorable sense of justice; but his method of exercising justice was eminently paternal. He regarded complaint against a magistrate as nothing less than treason. With his Council, the "Nine Men," he had one wrangle after another. Both the Nine Men and himself repeatedly sent protests to Holland, and the West India Company chose to

THE FERRY IN 1746

let the pugnacious Director and his people fight the thing out among themselves.

This indifference on the part of Holland, which plainly took nothing more than a commercial interest in the colony, naturally inspired little loyalty toward the home government. The nation that ignored their protests, let their fortifications crumble from lack of repair, and refused to guard them by proper numbers of soldiery, could expect no ardor of patriotism from those who were so treated.

Meanwhile trouble began to show itself between the Dutch and the Connecticut colony. The latter claimed authority over the English towns on Long Island, and threatened also to take possession of the Dutch settlements. The English were jealous of the rich territory of the Dutch. They beheld the valuable trade which had sprung up through the instrumentality of the Dutch West India Company. They were inclined to consider the Hollanders intruders. The English claimed the entire continent as their domain by virtue of the discovery made by their navigator, Cabot. Efforts were made to settle the disputes and differences, without success. All negotiations proved futile. With the Indians on one side and the English on the other the situation for the New Netherlands was perilous indeed. At last the Long Island towns, with Haarlem, New Amsterdam, and Bergen, assembled in convention and prepared a remonstrance to the home government, charging all their disasters to the lack of interest manifested by the mother country in their welfare. The colonists divided into two parties, one favoring adherence to Holland, the other favoring the acceptance of English rule.

In 1664 Charles II. granted to his brother James, the Duke of York and Albany, a patent of all the territory lying between the Connecticut River and Delaware Bay, in which was included the whole of the Dutch possessions. The Duke immediately dispatched four ships, with 450 soldiers, under command of his Deputy Governor, Colonel Richard Nicolls, to take possession of the territory. The squadron anchored at Nyack Bay, between New Utrecht and Coney Island, in August, 1664. The block house on Staten Island was captured, and all communication between Manhattan and the neighboring colonies was effectually intercepted.

The people were not prepared for this invasion. The very liberality the Dutch loyalists had exercised toward other nations was to seal their doom. The English settlers whom they had welcomed with open arms were anxious for a change of government, and the arbitrary conduct of the Dutch officials induced many of the Hollanders to coincide with the wishes of the English. Stuyvesant was powerless; the Fates were against him, and resistance was useless. Yet he would have refused to surrender, and was for making the best possible fight. But the people refused to rally under his leadership, and without the striking of a blow the Dutch colony fell under English rule.

CHAPTER VI

KINGS COUNTY AFTER THE ENGLISH CONQUEST
1665 – 1700

Assembly at Hempstead. The "Duke's Laws." Lovelace. New York Retaken by the Dutch. Colve becomes Governor. Return of English Rule under the Treaty of 1674. Dongan and the Popular Assembly. De Sille. Journal of Dankers and Sluyter. The Ferry. A Dutch Dinner. The Schoolmaster and the Constable. William and Mary and the Leisler Revolution. Sloughter appointed Governor. Execution of Leisler, and Subsequent Honors of a Public Reinterment. Long Island receives the name of Nassau. Development of Privateering. Captain Kidd visits and buries Treasure on Long Island. Bellomont and the Suppression of Piracy. First Trial for Treason.

WHEN Nicolls assumed control as Governor of New Amsterdam, under the patent to the Duke of York, he considered it best to act in a liberal spirit toward the Dutch, and endeavored to gain their good will and esteem. Indeed, this was the wise English policy which he represented. So conciliatory was his administration that the Dutch element did not appear to be affected by the change. The trade with Holland was continued without interruption. The Dutch were permitted to elect all minor officials and to observe the customs of the fatherland. New York received a new charter, and the government was placed in the hands of a Mayor, Aldermen, and Sheriff, appointed by the Governor. The legislative power was vested in the Governor and Council, who alone possessed the power to impose taxes.

The titles to property in the province were not in any way disturbed. The Council was careful to confirm and declare legal all grants, patents, and other evidences of title which had been derived through the Dutch government. New grants in confirmation were given, and additional expense in consequence was imposed upon the owners. Large sums were also expended in repairing the forts in and about the harbor to resist any attempt which might be made to retake the city.

Measures were also adopted to provide a more perfect and uniform system for the government of the towns on Long Island. In order to reconcile differences, and establish laws which should control in each town, Nicolls organized an Assembly of delegates, composed of representatives from each town. The Assembly thus formed, met in Hempstead in 1665. Breuckelen was represented in that body by two of her well-known citizens, in the persons of Frederick Lubbertsen and Evertsen Bout. The Assembly adopted a code of laws which were called the "Duke's Laws." Considering the state of the times and the varied conditions of the people, the code thus adopted was reasonable and just to all. These laws continued in operation with slight amendments until 1683, when Governor Dongan convened his provincial Assembly. The actions of Governor Nicolls gave the delegates satisfaction and pleasure, and they became his fast friends. They expressed their admiration of his actions by an address of congratulation to the Duke of York, which was characterized by an exceedingly deferential tone toward the new authority. Many of the people objected to the tone of this address, and gave vent to their feelings in outspoken language against the delegates. So fearless and indiscreet was the language used, and so imminent did the violence threatened by the anti-English element appear, that the Government was constrained to take notice of the same. At a court held in 1666, a stringent act was passed to prevent a repetition of the slanders against the delegates.

In 1665, Long Island, with Staten Island, was created a shire, and called Yorkshire, as a token of respect to the proprietor, the Duke of York. The shire thus formed was divided into districts, which were denominated ridings. The towns included in Kings County, Staten Island, and Newtown, were called the West Riding. Nicolls displayed much wisdom in the management of the colony, and thereby won the respect of the people. He did not, however, remain long in service. Being anxious to return to Europe, in 1668 he bade farewell to the New World, and set his face eastward. Upon his return to his native land he engaged in his country's service in the war with Holland, and gave his life in defending the flag in a naval engagement in 1692.

Nicolls was succeeded by Governor Francis Lovelace, whose administration was a striking contrast to that of his predecessor. Despotic, arrogant, and self-willed, Lovelace was born to be a "paternal" ruler, and ever manifested a domineering spirit. The inhabitants had always claimed the right to levy and impose their own taxes, and protested against taxation without representation. To all protests he paid no attention except to "pronounce their complaints as scandalous and seditious." His frequent remark was, "the people should have liberty for no thought but how to pay their taxes." In order to carry out his views, and to display his power, he imposed a duty of ten per cent. upon all imports and exports arriving at or going from the province.

In 1672, Charles II., instigated by the French, proclaimed war against Holland. This rupture led the Dutch to conceive the idea of regaining their lost possessions. A squadron consisting of five vessels was fitted out, and placed under the command of Admirals Beuckes and Evertson. The fleet thus prepared sailed from Holland and appeared off Sandy Hook on the 29th of July, 1673. The news of the expedition reached the city long before the arrival of the fleet. Governor Lovelace had no adequate idea of the importance and necessity of preparation to resist the attack. He left the city and proceeded to Albany to regulate the difficulties with the Indians, and placed the fort in charge of Captain Manning. When the news reached the city that the Dutch fleet was approaching, Manning sent messengers to Governor Lovelace, requesting him to return speedily. He came, and at once commenced active defensive preparations. The fort was manned, and soldiers were mustered into service and drilled. The enemy not appearing, the Governor disbanded his forces and went to Connecticut. When the fleet reached Sandy Hook, Manning again informed the Governor and requested him to return, and in the mean time employed himself in collecting recruits. He was not successful. The love of fatherland could not be obliterated from the hearts of Dutchmen. They refused to volunteer against their own flesh and blood, and instead spiked the guns of the fort to prevent any resistance to the fleet. The soldiers in the fort were but amateurs, and having had no experience were of but little service. The fleet anchored in New York Bay, July 30, 1673.

Manning lacked courage, and did not possess any attribute fitting him to properly defend the city. In his dilemma, and not having the aid and assistance of the Governor, he found himself powerless to act as the occasion demanded. He sent a messenger to the fleet to inquire their object in disturbing the peace of the colony. In the morning, the admirals dispatched an officer to demand the immediate surrender of the fort. Manning, anxious to gain time, requested that he might have until the following day to give his answer.

This was refused, and he was notified that unless the city was surrendered in half an hour the fort would be bombarded. To this notification no reply was received. The Dutch, true to their word, commenced a cannonade which resulted in killing and wounding a number of men. The salute of hot shot was not returned. Captain Colve, with a band of six hundred men, landed, and the attacking force was ranged in line of battle in front of the fort, and prepared to make a triumphal march through the city. Manning became agitated and frightened. He commenced negotiations, but, as he had no power to enter into any agreement, he was compelled to surrender.

The city, again in the possession of its original settlers, was called New Orange, and the fort was named Fort Hendrick. Some of the English soldiers taken as hostages of war were sent to Holland.

It may well be supposed that this successful capture produced a deep sense of mortification to the English Government and the New England colonies. Manning was subsequently court-martialed and tried for cowardice and treachery. His defense was mainly that he had no time to put the fort in a proper condition of defense — that the enemy were eight hundred strong, while he had but eighty men in the fort, and that he sought to delay capitulation, hoping that help might arrive. He was found guilty by the court. Through the influence of friends his life was spared, but he was compelled to suffer the ignominy of having his sword broken over his head by the executioner in front of the City Hall, and he was declared incapable of ever holding any office, either civil or military, in the gift of the Crown. Governor Lovelace also was severely reprimanded, and all his property was confiscated to the Duke of York. It would appear that the conduct of the Governor was more reprehensible than that of Manning. Manning was merely a subaltern, and Lovelace being Governor, it was his duty to exercise proper care in defending the territory committed to his control. He was twice notified by Manning of the intended attack, and seemed by his actions either to manifest but little interest, or not to realize the importance of defensive measures.

Captain Colve now assumed control of public affairs. Fearing that the English might endeavor to regain the territory, he repaired and strengthened the fort, and put the city under military protection. A new charter was given to the city, and the old forms of government readopted. Courts were established at various points, and all the magistrates were required to appear at New Orange, and swear allegiance to the Dutch Government.

Colve received his commission as Governor of the New Netherlands from the admiral of the fleet. He was very energetic, fortifying weak points, and asserting the claim of the Dutch to all the territory which Governor Stuyvesant had controlled. The fort was repaired in a substantial manner, and every precaution taken to effectually resist any attack which might be made. Colve directed that the provisions of the city should be securely kept, and prohibited the exportation of wheat and grain. In order to prepare the people for active service, he organized companies and had them drilled daily by competent officers in the manual of arms. The city under his administration assumed a military appearance. Parades and drills were of daily occurrence. The city was carefully guarded by watchmen ever on the alert.

While Governor Colve exercised authority in the province, he took occasion to visit Flatbush with his officials, where by his direction the magistrates of the various towns on Long

Island had assembled. He conveyed to them the intelligence that troops were on the way from New England to assail the town, and that it was necessary to make preparations for resistance. He commanded them to hold themselves in readiness to proceed to the city whenever he should require their presence. Many of the people considering it prudent to move to the city for safety, obtained permission to do so, and the Governor appointed a committee to secure proper accommodations for them.

A general exodus from Breuckelen and the other towns was the result. The inhabitants of the west end of the Island were eager to move, and in order to prevent depopulation, Governor Colve issued another order, stating that it was necessary for a portion of the males to remain in the towns to protect property and prevent invasion, and he directed that one third of the military force should remain.

The Dutch during their control of New York won for themselves the respect of all onlookers. In their management of the colony, notwithstanding many defects, they were more liberal than any of their neighbors. They were a hard-working, painstaking, thrifty class of people, whose sterling virtues have left upon the character of New York an impress that can never be obliterated. The character and principles of the Dutch, handed down from one generation to another, have done much to mould the great western commercial centre into the cosmopolitan metropolis it is to-day. The Knickerbocker patience and perseverance under trials, the honesty and integrity of the Dutch, their love of education and independence have been of incalculable value to the State and nation.

The Dutch were not to be surprised by any English force. The difficulty was settled by the treaty of peace between the States-General and England, signed at Westminster on the 9th of February, 1674. The terms of the treaty provided for the restoration of New York to the English. This was accomplished on the 10th of November, 1674, when the fort was surrendered to Major Edward Andros, the Governor appointed by the Duke of York.

Thus New York again passed from the control of the original settlers into the hands of their conquerors. The fort again assumed the name of Fort James, and the city resumed the name of New York. The inhabitants were required to swear allegiance to the King of England, and the form of government established by the English was restored.

Governor Andros also restored the titles, grants, and privileges which the towns had enjoyed under the English Government, and furthermore declared all legal proceedings which had been taken during the reoccupation by the Dutch to be legal and valid.

Andros was arbitrary and oppressive in his conduct, and did all in his power to prevent efforts on the part of the inhabitants to obtain representation in the councils of the government. In 1680, charges were preferred against him in which he was accused of interfering with the privileges of New Jersey, and he was summoned to England to answer. He was acquitted, and returned to be still more oppressive. In 1683, he was removed, and Colonel Thomas Dongan was appointed his successor, with directions to convene a popular assembly.

This Assembly was composed of the Governor, Council, and seventeen members elected by the people, and held a session commencing October 17, 1683, which lasted seventeen days. The Assembly adopted wise measures, which were called "the charter of liberties." This charter provided that the supreme authority should be vested in the Governor, Council, and Legislature elected triennially by the people. The right of trial by a jury of twelve men was guaranteed, and the liberty of the citizens was secured. Protection and freedom of religious belief were also assured.

The County of Kings was organized, and comprised the five towns of Breuckelen, Bushwick, Flatlands, Flatbush, and New Utrecht. Queens County was also organized. The province was divided into counties. These counties were: New York, Kings, Queens, Suffolk, Richmond, Westchester, Dutchess, Orange, Ulster, and Albany. In each county a court of sessions was to meet twice a year, and the Court of Oyer and Terminer annually. The offices of assessor and supervisor were also created.

The first town clarke (as it was then spelt) of which there is any record was Heer Nicasius De Sille.[1] He was appointed in 1671, and

[1] When, in 1660, it was deemed necessary to prepare defenses for Breuckelen and New Utrecht against attacks from the Indians, De Sille was directed to make the necessary surveys. Under Stuyvesant De Sille held the important position of attorney-general. He was a man of ability and influence. The position he held under Stuyvesant demonstrated the fact that his attainments were appreciated. He was born in Arnheim. His ancestors were natives of Belgium, who fled to Holland to escape religious persecution, and whose devotion to the interests of their adopted country was manifested on many occasions in the noble stand taken by the Dutch Republic to maintain its independence against the Spanish invasion. He came to New Netherland in 1653, commissioned by the West India Company to reside at New Amsterdam, and by his counsel aid and assist the Governor in his duties. He was directed

acted in that capacity for four years. Michil Hainelle succeeded him in 1675, and held office until 1690. During the administration of De Sille, Frederick Lubbertsen and Peter Perniedeau were trustees and overseers. In 1676 we find Teunis G. Bergen and Thomas Lambertsen filling the offices of trustee and overseer.

Of New York and Brooklyn immediately after the establishment of English rule we find some interesting glimpses in the journal of Jasper Dankers and Peter Sluyter, published in the collections of the Long Island Historical Society.[1] These two Dutch travelers were members of the sect founded by Jean de Labadie, and known as Labadists. The Labadists had found shelter in tolerant and enlightened Amsterdam when persecuted in France. The new faith was embraced by many of the Walloons at Rotterdam and elsewhere. A

---

to give his advice on all subjects relating to the interests of the colony. It is said that he built the first house in New Utrecht. It was at his house that the brave General Woodhull, the hero of Long Island, who gave his life for his country, breathed his last. — S. M. O.

[1] *Journal of a Voyage to New York and a Tour in Several of the American Colonies in* 1679–80. By Jasper Dankers and Peter Sluyter of Wiewerd, in Friesland. Translated from the original manuscript in Dutch for the Long Island Historical Society, and edited by Henry C. Murphy, Foreign Corresponding Secretary of the Society. Brooklyn, 1867.

community, resembling in many respects those of the Quakers, was established at Wiewerd, and the promoters resolving upon colonization in America, Dankers and Sluyter were sent to New York on a tour of investigation. After their first tour, of which their journal speaks, they were again sent to New York in 1683, to establish a colony.

The Labadists give a detailed account of their experiences in New York and on Long Island. They make a natural comment on the name "river" for the strait separating Long Island and Manhattan Island. "There is a ferry, . . . for the purpose of crossing over it, which is farmed out by the year, and yields a good income, as it is a considerable thoroughfare, this island being one of the most populous places in this vicinity."

The ferry at this time was patronized by both white men and Indians, though the Indians usually economized by using their own boats in carrying to New York their fish, fowl, or furs. The fare on the ferry was "three stuivers in zeewan for each person." A "stuiver in zeewan" was equivalent to less than half a cent of our money.

Going up the hill from the ferry the travelers passed through the "first village called

Breuckelen," in which they saw "a small and ugly little church standing in the middle of the road." Here they turned off to the right and reached Gowanus, where they were entertained by Simon Aertsen De Hart. After speaking of the large and remarkable oysters, "fully as good as those in England, and better than those we eat at Falmouth," the travelers give this description of the Dutch dinner: "We had for supper a roasted haunch of venison, which he had bought of the Indians for three guilders and a half of seewant, that is, fifteen stuivers of Dutch money [fifteen cents], and which weighed thirty pounds. The meat was exceedingly tender and good, and also quite fat. It had a slight spicy flavor. We were also served with wild turkey, which was also fat and of a good flavor; and a wild goose that was rather dry. Everything we had was the natural production of the country." The guest adds: "We saw here, lying in a heap, a whole hill of watermelons, which were as large as pumpkins, and which Symon was going to take to the city to sell. . . . It was very late at night when we went to rest in a Kermis bed, as it is called, in the corner of the hearth, alongside of a good fire."

These visitors did not entertain a very warm

appreciation for what the journal describes as "a miserable rum or brandy which had been brought from Barbadoes and other islands, and which is called by the Dutch *kill-devil.* All these people," continues the same narrator, "are very fond of it, and most of them extravagantly so, although it is very dear and has a bad taste." At New Utrecht, however, they drank "some good beer a year old."

The writers comment upon Coney Island in these words: "It is oblong in shape, and is grown over with bushes. Nobody lives upon it, but it is used in winter for keeping cattle, horses, oxen, hogs, and others, which are able to obtain there sufficient to eat the whole winter, and to shelter themselves from the cold in the thickets."

The Fort Hamilton region, called Najack (Nyack), after the Indian tribe of this name living in the vicinity, is spoken of as an island, it being surrounded by a marsh.

These and other records of the period indicate how little the early influence of the English rule affected the Dutch manners and customs, particularly on Long Island. The new rulers might introduce the English system of weights and measures, and adopt a new nomenclature for officials and civic systems, but for a long time, and far into the eighteenth century, Dutch life on Long Island remained singularly like all that it had been in the fatherland and in the pioneer homes.

An annual fair was established in Breuckelen in 1675. It was provided that there shall be kept "a ffayre and market at Breucklin, near the ffery, for all grain, cattle, or other products of the country, too be held on the ffirst Munday, Tusday, and Wenesday inn November, and in the City off New York the Thursday, Ffriday, and Saturday following."

To meet the necessary expenses of possible war, it was ordered that in case there should happen a war with the Indians, for the better carrying on of the same, one or more rates should be levied as there shall be occasion, an account whereof to be given to the following Court of Assizes.

At the same time it was ordered "that in all cases the magistrates through the whole government are required to do justice to the Indians as well as to the Christians."

In 1675, by reason of the fact that Long Island and Staten Island were separated by water, it was provided that Staten Island should have jurisdiction of itself, and be no longer dependent on the courts of Long Island, nor on the "Milishay."

The overseers and trustees were required to take an oath to administer the laws, without favor, affection or partiality to any person or cause, and, when required, to attend to the private differences of neighbors and endeavor to effect a reconciliation.

Slight allusion has heretofore been made to the schoolmaster. He was an important element in the community. As his labors were various, and much more irksome than at the present time, the following agreement, executed by the schoolmaster at Flatbush, in 1682, will be read with interest:

Article 1. The school shall begin at 8 o'clock, and goe out att 11; shall begin again att 1 o'clock and ende at 4. The bell shall be rung before the school begins.

2. When school opens one of the children shall reade the morning prayer as it stands in the catachism, and close with the prayer before dinner; and in the afternoon the same. The evening school shall begin with the Lord's prayer, and close by singing a Psalm.

3. He shall instruct the children inn the common prayers, and the questions and answers off the catachism, on Wednesdays and Saturdays, too enable them to saye them better on Sunday in the church.

4. He shall be bound to keepe his school

nine months in succession from September to June, one year with another, and shall always be present himself.

5. Hee shall bee chorister of the church, ring the bell three times before service, and reade a chapter of the Bible in the church, between the second and third ringinge of the bell; after the third ringinge, hee shall reade the ten commandments, and the twelve articles of ffaith, and then sett the Psalm. In the afternoon, after the third ringinge of the bell, hee shall reade a short chapter or one of the Psalms of David, as the congregation are assemblinge; afterward he shall again sett the Psalm.

6. When the minister shall preach at Broockland or Utrecht, hee shall bee bounde to reade from the booke used for the purpose. He shall heare the children recite the questions and answers off the catachism on Sunday and instruct them.

7. He shall provide a basin of water for the baptisme, ffor which he shall receive 12 stuyvers in wampum for every baptisme ffrom parents or sponsors. Hee shall furnish bread and wine ffor the communion att the charge of the church. He shall also serve as messenger for the consistorie.

8. Hee shall give the funerale invitations and toll the bell, and ffor which he shall receive ffor persons of 15 years of age and up-

wards, 12 guilders, and ffor persons under 15, 8 guilders; and iff he shall cross the river to New York, he shall have four guilders more.

The school money was paid as follows:

1. Hee shall receive ffor a speller or reader 3 guilders a quarter, and ffor a writer 4 guilders ffor the daye school. In the evening, 4 guilders ffor a speller and reader, and 5 guilders ffor a writer per quarter.

2. The residue of his salary shall bee 400 guilders in wheat (off wampum value), deliverable at Brookland ffery, with the dwellinge, pasturage, and meadowe appertaining to the school.

Done and agreede on inn consistorie inn the presence of the Honourable Constable and Overseers this 8th day of October, 1682.

Constable and Overseers.	The Consistorie.
CORNELIUS BERRIAN,	CASPARUS VANZUREN,
RYNIERE AERTSEN,	Minister,
JAN REMSEN,	ADRIAEN RYERSE,
	CORNELIS BAREN VANDERWYCK.

I agree to the above articles and promise to observe them.

JOHANNES VAN ECKKELLEN.

In those days the duties of a constable in Brooklyn were not confined to the present requirements. In 1670, a law was enacted, whereby his duties were defined. As the order is peculiar, it is here inserted: —

"Ordered that the constable of the towne of Breucklyne doe admonish the inhabitants too instruct theire children and servants, in matters of religione and the laws of the country.

"Ordered that the constable doe appoynte a suytable person too recorde every man's particular marke, and see such man's horse and colt branded.

"Ordered that the overseers and the constable doe paye the value off an Indyan coat ffor each woolf killed, and they cause the woolf's heade to be nayled over the doore of the constable, theire to remayne, and alsoe to pull off both eayres inn token that the heade is boughte and payed ffor."

In 1695 the Court of Sessions of Kings County "ordered that the constables of this towne shall on Sundaye or Sabbath daye tayke lawe ffor the apprehending off all Sabbath breakers, searche all ale houses, taverns, and other suspectede places ffor all prophaners and breakers off the Sabbath daye, and bringe them before the justice too bee dealt with accordinge to lawe."

As a penalty for refusing so to do, it was

further " ordered thatt ffor every neglect or deefault the constable shall paye a fine of six shillings."

At the same session it was "ordered that mad James bee kepte by Kings County in general and thatt the deacons of each towne within the sayde county doe fforthwith meete together and consider about theire proportions ffor the maintenance of sayde James."

Disputes having occurring between Brooklyn and Flatbush relative to their boundary or town lines, reference was had to the Court of Sessions and action was had thereon, as will appear by the record of its proceedings:

" Att a Cort of Sessions held ffor the West Riddinge of Yorkshire, uppon Long Island, the 18th day of December, 1677, the following order was mayde: There being some difference between the towns of Fflackbush and Brucklyne conserninge theire boundes, the which they are both willing to reffer to Captain Jacques Cortelyou and Captain Richard Stilwell too decyde, the Cort doe approve thereoff, and order theire report too bee determinative."

These Commissioners took five years and a half to perform their labors, and then reported the result of their deliberations, as follows :—

To the Worshippful Cort of Sessions nowe sitting at Gravesende, June 21, 1683:

These maye certiffie thatt inn obedience too an order ffrom sayde Cort and bye consente of bothe townes of Breucklyn and Ffackbush, too run the lyne twixt the sayde townes, which are wee underwritten, have done and markt the trees twixt towne and towne, as witness our hands the daye and yeare above written.

JACQUES CORTELYOU,
RICHARD STILLWELL.

The surveyor, Philip Wells, gave his certificate that he found the line run by the Commissioners to be just and right. These certificates were recorded by order of the court.

In 1671 one Thomas Lambertsen and wife sued John Lowe for defamation of character. The defendant confessed that he was drunk, " and was verry sorry for defaminge the plaintiff's wife," and begged his pardon in open court. They " ordered him to paye the costs off the plaintiff's attendance, and keepe a civill tongue in his heade."

Some of the orders made by the Court of Sessions, as contained in the ancient records, are very interesting at this period, and express in a great measure the character of the early settlers : —

"At a Court of Sessions held at Gravesend the 16th day of June by His Majesty's authority in the twenty-first year of the reign of our Sovereign Lord Charles the second, by the Grace of God of Great Britaine, Ffrance and Ireland, King, Defender of the ffaith, in the year of our Lord, 1662. Present: Mathias Nichols, Esquire, President; Mr. Cornelis Van Ruyter, Captain; John Manning, Mr. James Huddard, and Mr. Richard Betts, Justices.

"Weras during this Court of Sessions their have been several misdemeanors committed in contempt of authority in the towne of Gravesende, by one throwing down the stocks, pulling down of fences and such like crimes; the court also find that there was noe watch in the town which might have prevented itt, and being the offenders cannot be discovered, itt is ordered that the towne stand fined five pounds till they have made discovery of the offenders."

The penalty in slander cases was very light, as appears by a verdict rendered in an action for defamation in 1699. The verdict was as follows: "At a cort of General sessions, held att Gravesende, December 1, 1669, John Ffurman, plf., vs. Adraiaen Ffrost, def't. The Plaintiff declared in an action of defamacon, how that the defendant reported him to be a purjured person, and common lyer, which was sufficiently proved, and also confessed by the defendant. The Jury brought in the verdict for the plaintiff, with five pounds damages and costs."

Among the measures marking the progress of the county was a provision by which all the highways in the region were to be laid out four rods wide.

When, in 1685, the Duke of York succeeded to the throne of England under the title of James II., he instructed Governor Dongan to assert the prerogative of the Crown as a natural right, to impose taxes, and also prohibited the establishment of printing presses in the colony. He was opposed to the diffusion of information, and evidently thought that education and knowledge would weaken and destroy his power over the people. Thus, selfishness marked his whole course. In August, 1685, the provincial council was dissolved by order of the Governor, and no other was chosen or summoned. This course was adopted to lessen the influence of the people, and concentrate the entire management and control in the hands of the Governor.

On the 3d of May, 1686, an important event occurred for Brooklyn. It was the issuance of a patent whereby all the rights and privileges granted by Governor Nichols in 1667 were fully confirmed and ratified. Dongan, in the same year, also granted a charter to the city of New York, confirming the franchises previously granted to the corporation, and placed the government upon a solid foundation. The Governor, however, still retained the appointment of mayor, under-sheriff, clerk, and all other important officials, merely giving the people the right to choose their aldermen, assistant aldermen, and minor officials, at an annual election to be held on St. Michael's day. This patent of 1686 was a very important document for New York City. Upon this document New York based its claims to ownership in the Brooklyn shore. It was this charter which made sailors on board of United States vessels at the Brooklyn Navy Yard citizens of New York City, and gave them the right to vote in the seventh ward of New York.

Dongan was a fast friend of the Indians, and during his administration secured their good will by counsel and assistance. He had their confidence, and in various ways they manifested gratitude. They called him the "white father," and he was long held in remembrance by the savage tribes, who appreciated his many kind acts to them. He succeeded better with the Indians than he did with the whites.

The King was anxious to introduce the Catholic religion, in opposition to the wishes of the colonists. The feeling between the two parties formed as a result of this threat became very bitter. Dongan quickly saw that the policy of intolerance would jeopardize the perpetuity and peace of the English possessions, and opposed the measure. The Crown officers appointed by the home government were all Catholics, and in order to appease popular prejudices, Dongan selected his councilors from among the best known and foremost Protestants. This judicious policy was not approved by the King, and in 1688 Dongan was recalled, and Francis Nicholson assumed the management of affairs.

In the mean time, Sir Edward Andros had been appointed royal governor of New England and New York. Nicholson, as his deputy, acted during his absence. The troubles which assailed the people in consequence of the arbitrary acts of the King were not to last long. The hour of deliverance was at hand. The dismal forebodings of the people were removed when the intelligence was received that the King had abdicated his throne, and that the reign of William and Mary had begun. This was in 1689. The citizens of New York thereupon assumed the power to remove and depose all the officials who had been appointed through the instrumentality of the late king. The authority of Deputy Nicholson was questioned. Each sovereign had adherents. Parties were formed among the people. One sustained the late sovereign, while another supported the new potentates. Political and religious discussion waxed warm, and the two parties became known as the democratic and aristocratic classes. Some maintained that the change of sovereigns in no way affected the colonial government, and that the commissions granted by James were valid until set aside and declared illegal by the new power. Others considered the change in England as a complete revolution, which extended to every province belonging to the kingdom. They held that all things were in a state of anarchy, and that no one possessed the power to control; that all officials were *functus officio*, and consequently the power rested with the people, and that they alone could devise measures or means of government, until the sovereign will should be expressed.

As a result of this condition of affairs the inhabitants of Long Island deposed their magistrates and elected others to fill the places of those they had removed. They also took occasion to send a large body of militia to New York to aid the popular party in that city, which was led by Jacob Leisler. He held the position of captain, was an old, wealthy, and respected citizen, a firm Protestant, and an opponent of the Catholics. The public money was deposited in the Fort, and the people were anxious to secure its control. A detachment of forty-seven men repaired to the Fort, obtained possession without resistance, and Captain Leisler became the acknowledged and recognized leader of the revolutionary movement. He assumed control in behalf of the new sovereigns, and at once took measures to protect the public property. The defenses were strengthened, and a battery of six guns erected. The erection of this battery was the beginning of the public park long known as the Battery.

As everything was in a chaotic state, it was deemed advisable to organize a Committee of Safety, whose first act was to place the city under the command of Leisler. Subsequently the authority of Leisler was confirmed by a dispatch directed to the late Governor, or to such other persons as might be in command, requiring such person to assume the entire control of governmental affairs. Thereupon Leisler took the title of Lieutenant-Governor, and appointed his advisory council, consisting of eight well-known citizens, to aid him in the discharge of his trust. Having entire and complete supremacy, he resolved to place the city in an orderly condition, and to accomplish this purpose took active measures. His conduct did not please the people. Some were jealous of his power, and began to stir the people into rebellion. This was accomplished with but little effort, and resulted in a street riot, from which the Governor barely escaped with his life. The services of the militia were called in requisition, and for a short time the result was uncertain. The riot, however, was subdued. Several of the ringleaders were captured, thrown into prison, and a court summoned to try them for treason. The chief leader, Nicholas Bayard, was kept in the cells of the City Hall for a period of fourteen months, until released by Governor Sloughter.

In 1691, General Henry Sloughter was appointed Governor by the sovereign authority. Upon his arrival he demanded the surrender of the Fort, which at first was refused. Major Ingolsby, who had been appointed by him Lieutenant-Governor, at once landed his forces and blockaded the Fort. In this work Ingolsby was aided and urged on by the enemies of Leisler. For seven weeks the city was kept in this state. Leisler refused to surrender his authority until the commission of the new governor was produced. At the same time, however, he declared himself willing to surrender possession to any one duly authorized and deputed to take his place. Ingolsby, still urged on by Leisler's foes, did all he could to irritate and annoy him.

On the 19th of March, 1691, Sloughter was met by a delegation consisting of Philipse Van Courtland and others, representing the anti-Leislerian party, which expressed to him a cordial greeting and loyalty. With his escort from the city he proceeded to the City Hall, exhibited his commission, and took the oath of office. It was late at night when he reached the Hall, and although it was near midnight he dispatched Ingolsby and a party of soldiers, at the instigation of Van Courtland and his friends, to demand a surrender of the Fort. Leisler was suspicious, and thinking that all was not right, refused to surrender, and sent a letter by one of his men who had known Sloughter, with directions to ascertain if he was really present and had issued the order, or whether it had been prepared by some one who had assumed the rôle of authority. This act angered Sloughter, and he at once told the messenger that he intended to make himself known in New York. Major Ingolsby was again directed to return and take possession of the Fort, and to release Bayard and the other prisoners who had been committed by Leisler for treason. Upon their release and restoration to freedom they were elevated to the position of members of the Council. This augured ill for Leisler. The new Governor summoned Leisler and his son-in-law, Milburne, to appear before him without delay. Leisler refused to give up possession and still held the Fort. He, however, sent Milburne and Delanoy to the Governor to obtain the assurance that his life would be spared. The messengers sent to make terms were imprisoned, and another demand was made to surrender. Leisler became frightened; matters were becoming exceedingly hot and disagreeable. Resistance could not be kept up much longer, and he feared his life would be forfeited in consequence of his disobedience to the lawfully constituted authority. He deeply felt the necessity of reconciliation, and sent a letter of apology to the Governor for holding the Fort. He admitted that his action had been unwise, and excused himself on the ground that he feared the people would take his life if he gave up control to Ingolsby. This letter was treated with contempt, receiving no consideration at the hands of the Governor or his Council. Sloughter convened his Council at the City Hall. All of its members were enemies of Leisler. Leisler, deserted by the soldiers of the Fort, was brought a prisoner before Sloughter, and imprisoned with several others in the guard-house.

At this meeting of the Council the Governor appointed John Lawrence Mayor of New York.

Leisler with his fellow prisoners remained in the guard-house four days, when the Governor and Council again met to consider the propriety of his removal to prison. On the following day a court was organized to try the prisoners for murder and rebellion. The court met on the 30th day of March. Leisler refused to put in any plea, maintaining that the court had no jurisdiction of the case; that the sovereigns alone had the right to decide whether he had acted without legal authority. The judges were unwilling to assume the power to decide the question, and submitted it to the Governor and Council, who held that the point was not well taken. Thereupon Leisler was found guilty on the 13th day of April, declared to be a usurper, and with Milburne was condemned to death.

The Governor did not at once sign the death warrant. He was not satisfied with the situation, and feared to incur the displeasure of the King. The enemies of Leisler urged him to the act, without success. At last, after a month had passed away, they adopted a new method to gain their desire. A feast was prepared, to which the Governor was invited. They again urged upon him his duty in the matter, and at last by the use of flattery, and while the Governor was under the influence of the good wine which had been provided for the occasion, succeeded in their endeavor.

The anti-Leislerian party, having accomplished the desire of their hearts, could not rest until the warrant was put into execution. They feared that the Governor might relent and revoke his order. Nicolls, Van Courtland, Bayard, and those of their adherents who had been imprisoned by the direction of Leisler, were burning for vengeance, and nothing but his ignominious death would allay their fury.

The warrant having been signed, the festal board lost its attractions. An officer took possession of the document and carried it to the City Hall. Orders were issued to lead out the prisoners to instant execution. In order to keep the matter from the ears of Sloughter, some remained at the entertainment and kept the Governor in good humor and forgetfulness with wine. The day of execution was cold and dismal. In the drizzling rain the prisoners were led out to meet their fate. The scaffold was erected in the park opposite the City Hall. Friends of Leisler gathered round him in the trying hour, bewailing the doom of their leader, and in bitter words execrated those who had sought and obtained the death warrant. Leisler lamented the fate of his son-in-law, and with his dying breath addressed his son and friend in words of tenderness. Turning to Milburne he said: "Why must you die? You have been but a servant doing my will. What I have done has been in the service of my King and Queen, for the Protestant cause and for the good of my country;

for this I must die. Some errors I have committed; for these I ask forgiveness, and I entreat my children to do the same."

Thus perished the last Dutch Governor of New York.[1] His remains were interred in his own ground near the location of old Tammany Hall. The treatment he received was unjust. He had assumed the reins of government at the behest of the people, when they had no ruler, and continued to act in that capacity, considering the open letter of the new sovereigns as a sufficient authorization. He was condemned unheard, receiving the

---

[1] "No man has been more maligned or misunderstood than Jacob Leisler. Historians have deliberately misjudged him, drawing their conclusions from the biased reports of the few aristocrats who hated or the English officials who despised him. Jacob Leisler was one of the earliest of American patriots. His brief and stormy career as Provincial Governor of New York was marked by mistakes of judgment, but his mistakes were more than overbalanced by his foresight and statesmanship. He acted as one of the people for the people. He summoned a popular convention, arranged the first mayoralty election by the people, attempted the first step toward colonial union by endeavoring to interest the several provinces in a continental congress, and sought to cripple the chief adversary of the English in America, France, by the masterly stroke of an invasion of Canada. That he failed is due to the jealousy, the timidity, and the short-sightedness of his fellow colonists. But he builded wiser than he knew; for, though he died a martyr to colonial jealousy and English injustice, his bold and patriotic measures awoke the people to a knowledge of their real power, and prepared them for that spirit of resistance to tyranny which a century later made them a free republic." — Elbridge S. Brooks, *The Story of New York*, p. 74.

treatment of a common malefactor. It is but just to say of him that he resigned his authority to the new government as soon as the Council had been sworn in, and as soon as he was properly apprised of his supersedure. He was prejudged by a court composed of his enemies, some of whom, on account of malice, were not qualified to try him. In 1695 his estate, which had been confiscated, was restored to his family. Subsequently Parliament declared that Leisler had held under proper authority, set aside all acts of attainder and judgments which had been passed against him and his associates, and the bodies of Leisler and Milburne received the honor of a public reinterment. It was but tardy justice.

During Sloughter's administration many important changes were made. The government was placed upon a firm basis, and various courts were organized. Courts of Common Pleas and General Pleas were organized in every county, and the town governments assumed in a measure their present form. The number of supervisors was reduced to one from each town, with three surveyors of highways.

In May, 1691, the General Assembly confirmed all previous grants and patents. The grants to Breuckelen were thus again confirmed.

Governor Sloughter died suddenly July 23, 1691. Some supposed that he was poisoned by the friends of Leisler, whose bitterness was ever manifested toward him. The theory of poisoning, however, was not supported by the *post mortem* examination.

If religious questions had been at the bottom of the democratic revolt led by Leisler, the triumph of the aristocratic class did not close the religious differences.[1] Benjamin Fletcher, who succeeded Sloughter as Governor, was a man of limited education, narrow views, self-opinionated obstinacy, and always questionable personal sincerity. It was a darling project with him to introduce the English language and the Episcopalian forms of worship. To accomplish this purpose he made

[1] "The government of the colony was at once put on the basis on which it stood until the outbreak of the Revolution. There was a governor appointed by the king, and a council likewise appointed; while the assembly was elected by the freeholders. The suffrage was thus limited by a strict property qualification. Liberty of conscience was granted to all Protestant sects, but not to Catholics; and the Church of England was practically made the state church, though the Dutch and French congregations were secured in the rights guaranteed them by treaty. It was, then, essentially a class or aristocratic government, — none the less so because to European eyes the little American colony seemed both poor and rude." — Theodore Roosevelt, *New York*, p. 71.

strenuous efforts, bringing to bear every influence within his power. The Hollanders were wedded to their own peculiar forms of church government, and regarded their church as best entitled to be considered the established form of religious worship. Vigorous efforts were consequently made to retain its supremacy, and great opposition was manifested toward the proposed change. The Dutch language was long successfully retained in the Dutch churches. It was not until 1767 that the English language was introduced, causing great dissatisfaction among the old Knickerbocker stock. The tenacity displayed in retaining the language of the fatherland, and the refusal to provide English services, drove many young people into the Episcopalian fold. To this circumstance may be ascribed the reason why to-day so many Dutch families are found connected with that denomination. Had the fathers gratified the wishes of their children by providing services in the English language, the Reformed Dutch Church would have retained many families that found their way into the Episcopalian Church.

William Bradford, of Philadelphia, in 1693, established the first printing-press in New York City, and had the exclusive contract from the city government to print the laws, ordinances, and corporation advertising. He had no competitor, and must have enjoyed a rich harvest. To Bradford belongs the credit of establishing the first newspaper ever printed in the province. His effort in this direction proved eminently successful. The paper was first given to the public in 1725, and was called the "New York Gazette." At first it was merely a weekly paper, printed on a small half sheet, containing only two pages. As his business increased it was enlarged to four pages.

In 1693 Long Island received a new name, being designated as Nassau Island. The change met with but little favor, and although the name Nassau is intimately associated with the history of the island and with local institutions, it failed to become permanent.

During this period a system of privateering came into vogue, which in a great measure received encouragement from the authorities. The entire coast was infested by daring buccaneers and pirates, who plundered the shipping, making serious depredations upon the commerce of the country. The province suffered greatly from these freebooters, and, although complaint was made from time to time to the constituted authorities, no redress or protection was received. The officials themselves were corrupt, and participated in the profits derived from the nefarious and infamous business. Governor Fletcher fell under strong suspicion of complicity. Legitimate trade was destroyed, and many embarked in the new calling who under other circumstances could not have been induced to pollute themselves by engaging in so vile a traffic.

The English government at last became alarmed. Trade was suspended and merchants were afraid to send their vessels and wares over the ocean. They were unwilling to risk their property in so dangerous and hazardous an enterprise. It became necessary to adopt active means to suppress piracy. The Governor could not be trusted, and, in order to break up this evil, Governor Fletcher was recalled in 1695, and Lord Bellomont appointed in his stead.

Lord Bellomont did not enter upon the discharge of his duties until 1698. He was a man of quick perception, and was convinced that active measures were necessary. To carry out his views he urged the Government to equip an armed naval force to cruise in the western waters and capture the human sharks who were pillaging vessels and destroying the commerce of the nation. England at that time was engaged in a war with France, and had not the means or equipments to respond to the appeal. She required all her naval vessels to defend herself against her neighbor. Bellomont was determined to accomplish his laudable undertaking to destroy piracy in American waters, and, as he could receive no aid from the Crown, resolved to organize a stock company for the purpose. He was encouraged in his effort by the King, who approved the plan, and, with the Duke of Shrewsbury and others of the nobility, became a shareholder in the company thus formed. The object of the company was to build and man vessels to capture the pirates. A sum of money amounting to about $30,000 was raised. A fine and strong vessel called the Adventure Galley was placed in commission. She carried sixty sailors and mounted thirty guns.

Captain William Kidd, a bold and adventurous officer, was placed in command of the ship thus equipped. In order to encourage him in his labor, it was provided that his share in the enterprise should be one fifth of the proceeds. He was a man of large experience, having been engaged in the West Indian and New York trade for many years, and having at various times been employed as captain of packet ships. His experience and knowledge of the coast preëminently fitted him for the undertaking. He had lived in New York a long time, owned considerable property, and was looked upon as a man in every way worthy to discharge the duties assigned him. Bellomont and Robert Livingston had the utmost confidence in him, and gave him a warm recommendation for the position. He married a lady of high social rank in New York, and was privileged to move in the best circles of the city.

The vessel sailed under flattering auspices in April, 1699, from Plymouth, England, for New York. Arriving at the latter port, Captain Kidd shipped ninety additional men, and proceeded to the Indian seas in search of pirates. Kidd soon found that his own seamen sympathized with the buccaneers, and were far from unwilling to assume the rôle of pirates. It will never be known what arguments induced him to turn aside from the path of duty, and join the band of pirates he was sent to destroy. The fact is that he was led to abandon his enterprise, and became the most daring and bold robber on the sea that ever trod the quarter deck. Reckless and energetic, he soon enriched himself with booty taken from merchantmen upon the high seas. It is said that he would often return to the shores of New York and Long Island, and bury his ill-gotten gains for future use.

Kidd not only buried treasure on Long Island, but, if romantic traditions are to be believed, visited the island under certain sentimental conditions. He is credited with having made early visits to Bushwick in attendance upon a pretty young woman whose family resided in that region, and with having sought hospitality at the "Kickout," on the way to and from the home of the lady.

Even after the character of his undertakings became known, Kidd ventured to return to Long Island. After capturing a large frigate he landed at Gardiner's Island, and buried a quantity of treasure. After dividing some of the ill-gotten gains with his crew, he discharged them, and went to Boston to reside, under an assumed name, hoping that he would not be discovered. In this expectation he made a great mistake. A man like him could not pass long unnoticed. His past career rendered his detection sure. Bellomont was in Boston attending to certain affairs of state, and, meeting Kidd in the street, at once recognized him, and speedily caused his arrest. It was a proud and happy day for Bellomont, and proved to be a crowning effort in his life. His wish was accomplished! He had found and with his own hand arrested the notorious pirate. The prisoner was at once sent to England on a charge of murder and piracy, was tried, found guilty, and sentenced to death, and executed on the 12th of May, 1701. Kidd's family continued to reside in New York, feeling keenly the disgrace which had been brought upon them.[1]

Diligent search was now made for his buried treasures. A large quantity of valuable jewels and gold and silver was found at Gardiner's Island. The excitement on the subject became intense. Bellomont and Livingston, having recommended Kidd for appointment as commander of the expedition against the pirates, and in consequence of their former friendliness for Kidd, were accused unjustly of having connived at and participated in his

---

[1] There are varying views of Kidd's character and career. Thus Berthold Fernow writes in the *Narrative and Critical History of America* (vol. v. p. 195): "To-day that which was meted out to Kidd might hardly be called justice; for it seems questionable if he had ever been guilty of piracy."

spoils. Had this charge been true, Bellomont would hardly have been so ungrateful or imprudent as to arrest him in the streets of Boston and transport him to England for trial and execution.

Bellomont, in the administration of the affairs of state, allied himself with the democratic faction. Bayard, Van Courtlandt, and the other members of the Council who had opposed Leisler, were removed, and their places filled by the former adherents of Leisler. A new Assembly was called in May, 1699. Bellomont opened it with a speech calculated to please and encourage the people. He told them that he came with a firm determination to be just to all interests; that the public money should not be squandered by any one, and that all officials should be held to a strict accountability. The address gave satisfaction to the Assembly. Acts were passed for the suppression of piracy, regulating elections, and for the indemnification of those who had been excluded from the general pardon which had been previously granted. Bellomont instituted and initiated many reforms. Markets were erected at Coenties Slip, and at the foot of Broad Street. Streets were opened and paved, and provision was made for keeping them clean. A house was secured and used as a hospital for the sick poor of the city.

The ferry between Breuckelen and New York was leased for a period of seven years, and the rates of fare fixed. The fare for a single person was eight stuyvers in wampum, or a silver twopence; a shilling for a horse, twopence for a hog, and a penny for a sheep. By the terms of the lease the city of New York was to build a commodious ferry-house on the Breuckelen side, which was to be kept in repair by the ferryman.

The jurisdiction of Bellomont was enlarged by his appointment as Governor of Massachusetts as well as of New York. He was greatly interested in the Navigation Acts; but his efforts to enforce them were resisted by the residents and merchants of New England, and met with opposition in New York. The merchants of New York were incensed at his conduct, and made a vigorous complaint to the Board of Trade and Parliament. The matter, however, was never investigated, as he was released from trial, by the hand of death, in 1701.

In 1697, a mob of Kings County people, who resented the spirit of the English Government, assembled, " armed, at the Court House of Kings County, where they destroyed and defaced the King's arms which were hanging up there." Among those who so convened were the familiar names of John Rapalje, Jacob Ryerse, Garrett Cowenhoven, Jacob Bennett, and John Meserole, Jr.

In November, 1697, negroes were not allowed to be brought from New York on the Sabbath unless they were provided with passes. During the succeeding years similar legislation was enacted, and the liberty and freedom of the negro were still more restricted. He was "forbidden to run about on the Sabbath." The regulations with regard to the observance of the Sabbath were very stringent. One of the legislative enactments provided "that no people should pass on the Sabbath day unless it be to go to or from church, or other urgent and lawful occasions according to act of Assembly upon penalty of fine and imprisonment."

In 1693 one of the first trials for treason in the New World was held in Kings County. In those days petit magistrates, clothed with a little brief authority, became arbitrary, and often imagined that criticism and words uttered concerning the way they discharged their duties had a tendency to exasperate the people against the constituted authorities. They would often cause the arrest and confinement of citizens on frivolous and baseless charges, and denounce them as guilty of treason. Such a case was the trial of John Bibaut for "treason." The action taken by the justices clearly shows that it was a matter of but little moment, and fraught with no danger to the community. The following order shows the nature of the case: —

"October 11, 1693. Att a meeting of the Justices off Kings County, held att the County Hall.

"Present, Roetiff Martense, Nicholaus Stillwell, Joseph Hagerman, and Henry Ffilkin, Esquires, Justices.

"John Bibaut, off Brookland, inn the county aforesayde, wee aver being committed bye the said justices too the common jail of Kings County, ffor divers scandalous and abusive words spoken by the sayde John against theire majesties authority, and breache of the peace; the said John having now humbly submitted himself and craves pardon and mercy off the sayde justices ffor his misdemeanor, is discharged, paying the officers ffees, and being on his good behaviour, till the next cort of sessions inn November next ensuing the dayte thereoff."

Several others were arrested and imprisoned on similar charges made by the justices. Although the fines imposed were heavy, it is not to be presumed that the offenses committed were of a serious nature, as the accused were all discharged on payment of the fine exacted.

CHAPTER VII

BROOKLYN BEFORE THE REVOLUTION

1701-1775

Brooklyn becomes the Largest Long Island Settlement. Division of the Common Lands. Regulations as to the Cutting of Lumber. The King's Highway laid out. Brooklyn Officials at the Opening of the Century. Lord Cornbury's Proclamation to Long Island Justices. Slavery. Encroachments on the Common Highway. The trial of Zenger. Population in 1738. Fortifying Long Island. Newspaper Glimpses of pre-Revolutionary Life. Ferries. Kings County in the Assembly and the Provincial Convention. Philip Livingston. General Town Meeting in Brooklyn.

BEFORE the close of the seventeenth century Brooklyn had assumed a leading place among the Long Island towns. Indeed, in the number of assessed persons the village with the "ugly little church" began to exceed Midwout as early as 1675,[1] when it had sixty property owners who paid taxes.

At the beginning of the new century we

---

[1] The assessment rolls of the five Dutch towns in 1675 showed the following proportions in the number of persons assessed: Breuckelen, 60; Midwout, 54; Boswyck (Bushwick) 36; Amersfoort, 35; New Utrecht, 29.

find Breuckelen, if not growing rapidly as we now understand the term, at least treading steadily forward and assuming the traits of an organized community.

At a town meeting held in 1693, the common lands of Brooklyn had been divided as follows:

"All lands and woods, after Bedford and Cripplebush over the hills to the path of New Lotts, shall belong to the inhabitants of the Gowanis, beginning from Jacob Brower and soe to the uttermost bounds of the limitts of New Utrecht.

"And all the lands and woods that lyes betwixt the aforesaid path and the highway from the ferry toward Flattbush shall belong to the ffreeholders and inhabitants of Bedfford and Cripplebush.

"And all the lands that lyes in common after the Gowanis betwixt the limitts and bounds of Flattbush and New Utrecht shall belong to the ffreeholders and inhabitants of Breucklin, fred neck, the ferry and the Wallabout."

Among the commissioners appointed to lay out the common lands was Captain Henry Ffilkin, an influential resident of the town and an elder in the Reformed Church. The ordinance provided specifically as follows: "It is likewise ordered and agreed that Capt. Henry Falkin shall have a full share with any or all the ffreeholders aforesaid, in all the common lands or woods, in the whole patent of the Town of Broockland aforesaid beside a half share for his home lott. To have and to hold to him, his heirs and assigns forever. It is likewise ordered that no person whatsoever within the common woods, of the jurisdiction of Broockland aforesaid, shall cutt or fall any oak or chesnut saplings, for firewood during the space of four years from the date hereof, upon any of the said common lands or woods within the jurisdiction of Broockland patent, upon the penaltie of six shillings in money for every waggon load abovesaid soe cutt, beside the forfeiture of the wood soe cutt as abovesaid, the one half thereof to the informer, and the other half for the use of the poor of the Towne of Broockland aforesaid."

At a later town meeting[1] trustees were

---

[1] The peculiar methods employed by the citizens of Brooklyn at that time in electing their officials cannot be better illustrated than by the presentation of a report of one of those town meetings as follows: —

Att a towne meeting held this 29th day of April, 1699, at Breucklyn, by order of Justice Michael Hanssen ffor to chose town officers ffor to order all townes business and to deffend theire limits and bounds, and to lay out some part thereoff in lotts, to make lawes and orders ffor the best off the inhabitants, appointed for the common lands, and regulations adopted respecting the cutting of timber in the public woods. These rules were adopted to prevent the unnecessary cutting of timber and consequent waste. Among other things it was ordered "that no shoemaker or others shall cutt or ffall any trees to barke in the common woods, upon the penaltie of the payment of ffive pounds ffor every tree so cutt." It will be noticed that the orthography of that period was quite different from that in use in the present age.

The common woodlands, amounting to about 1550 acres,[1] were surveyed and apportioned, each house in town receiving an interest in the wood, and being provided with means of ingress and egress from the region so apportioned. A conveyance dated in 1705 gives "alsoe all the rights and privileges of the common woodlands of the town of Broockland aforesaid to said house belonging as per record of said town may appear."

and to raise a small tax ffor to defray the towne charges, now being or hereafter to come, to receive the townes revenues, and to pay the townes debts, and that with the advice off the justices off the said towne standing the space or time off two years. Chosen ffor that purpose by pluralitie of votes. Benjamin Vande Water, Joras Hanssen, Jan Garritse Dorlant.

By order off inhabitants aforesaid,

J. VANDE WATER, *Clarke.*

[1] Furman's *Notes*, p. 45.

When, in 1703, the improved fenced lands of Breuckelin were surveyed, it was found that Simon Aertson was the largest real estate owner, being the happy possessor of 200 acres.

On the 28th of March, 1704, Fulton Street, then called the King's Highway, was laid out by commissioners appointed by the General Assembly of the Province of New York. The commissioners to whom this duty was assigned were Joseph Hegeman, Peter Cortelyou, and Benjamin Vande Water.

The original plan or description of the road, being interesting and peculiar, is here inserted. It was as follows: —

"One publique, common and general highway, to begin from low water marke at the ferry in the township of Broockland, in Kings County, and from thence to run ffour rod wide up between the houses and land of John Aerson, John Coe and George Jacobs, and soe all along Broockland towne aforesaid, through the lane that now is, and ffrom thence straight along a certain lane to the southward corner of John Van Couwenhoven's land, and ffrom thence straight to Bedfford as it is now staked out, to the lane where the house of Benjamin Vandewater stands, and ffrom thence straight along through Bedfford towne to Bedfford lane, running between the lands of John Garretse Dorlant and Claes Burnse to the rear of the lands of the said Cloyse, and ffrom thence southerly to the old path now in use, and soe along said path to Philip Volkertses land, taking in a little slip of said Philip's land on the south corner, soe all along said road by Isaac Greg's house to the Fflackbush New Lotts ffence, and soe all along said ffence to the eastward, to the northeast corner of Eldert Lucas's land, lying within the New Lotts of Fflackbush aforesaid, being ffour rod wide, all along, to be and continue forever."

Jacob Vande Water, who became town clerk of Breuckelen in 1691, held the position until 1705, when he was succeeded by Henry Ffilkin. Ffilkin held office until 1714. From 1691 to 1699, Joris Hanssen, Hendrick Clausen, and Jan Gerbritse acted as trustees and commissioners of the town. In 1699, the trustees and commissioners were Benjamin Vande Water, Joris Hanssen, and John Garretse Dorlant. From 1700 to 1709, the trustees were Hendrick Vechte, Jacob Hanssen, and Cornelius Vanduyk.

The first supervisor of the town was Joris Hanssen, and he held the position from 1703 until 1714.

Jacob Vande Water, the clerk, owned property in the neighborhood of Tillary and Raymond streets. His tract was mentioned in the patent issued by Governor Dongan in 1686, ratifying previous grants. He took the oath of allegiance to the Government at the time his patent was ratified, having then resided in the colony twenty-nine years. In 1697, he was appointed one of the freeholders to lay out and divide the common lands, and acted in that capacity with Joris Hanssen and Jan Garretse Dorlant, heretofore referred to as trustees. Vande Water was a man of great importance in the little hamlet, and enjoyed the confidence of the community.

The officials of Brooklyn [1] who acted from 1700 were as follows: —

Hendrick Vechte was trustee from 1700 to 1726.

Jacob Hanssen was trustee from 1700 to 1708.

Cornelius Vanduyk was trustee from 1700 to 1726.

John Staats was trustee from 1709 to 1726.

Samuel Garritson (or Gerritse) was town clerk in 1714 and 1715.

---

[1] The total assessment value of real and personal estate in Brooklyn in 1706 was £3,122 12d, or about $15,610, and the tax on the same was £41 3s 7½d, or about $205. The tax levied in the County of Kings was £201 16s 1½d, or about $1,005.

Adrian Hegeman became town clerk in 1727, and served in that capacity until 1752.

Joramus Rapelye (Rapalje), Jacobus Leffertse, and Rem Remsen, acted as trustees from 1727 to 1752, a continuous and unbroken board.

Adrian Hegeman came from an old family, and was doubtless a son of Adriaen Hegeman, who, as schepen or schout in 1661, signed the petition to the Director-General of the Council of the New Netherlands, praying that assistance might be given to pay Carol Van Beauvois for teaching school, digging graves, running on errands as messenger, etc., referred to in a previous chapter. His salary as clerk was thirty-three and one third pounds per annum, or about $160 in our money.

On the death of Bellomont (in 1701) the administration devolved upon Lieutenant-Governor Nanfan, until the appointment of a new Governor. Nanfan at the time was temporarily absent in Barbadoes, and in consequence a sharp and bitter contest took place as to the management and control of the province. The anti-Leislerian party claimed that Colonel William Smith, being senior member of the Council, should exercise authority. The Leislerian or democratic party asserted that the same course should be pursued as at the time Sloughter died, which consisted in the election of a temporary chairman. The discussion waxed warm, and would have led to disastrous results, had not Lieutenant-Governor Nanfan opportunely arrived to quell the disturbance.

Nanfan was a strong exponent of the Leislerian policy, and warmly espoused that party's cause. The Assembly convened by him possessed his spirit, was actuated by the same motives, and enjoyed the confidence and support of Leisler's friends.

During the absence of Nanfan and while the Government was without a head, Peter Schuyler and Robert Livingston supported and sustained the pretensions of Colonel Smith, senior councillor, to be considered the temporary ruler of affairs. Livingston was one of Leisler's most determined enemies, and had been execrated as such by Milburne in his dying words. At this time Livingston held the very important office of Secretary of Indian Affairs and Collector of Customs. The new Assembly caused his removal, and required him to furnish his accounts for examination. Not being able to produce them, he was denounced and charged with being a defaulter. His expulsion from the Council followed, together with confiscation of his property and effects for the benefit of the province.

It seemed as if the enemies of Leisler were to be brought quickly to punishment, and that the martyr's friends were to enjoy the sweets of revenge. The feuds which existed between the two parties in the affairs of the colony produced the same confusion in the municipal affairs of the city. In the Board of Aldermen each party had its adherents, and the contentions between the two equaled in intensity of hate the feeling manifested between the contending parties in the war of the Rebellion. Some of the aldermen refused to take the oath of office at the hands of Mayor Noell, and he appointed others in their place. The friends of Leisler refused to act or to recognize the power of the Mayor to make new appointments. To enable an appeal to be taken to decide the question, the Aldermen took a recess, and the city was virtually without a government for a month. The court to whom the matter was referred held that the Mayor possessed the authority to act in the premises by filling vacancies, and thereupon the new officials took their seats. The Board thus became equally divided between the two parties.

The Mayor belonged to the aristocratic or anti-Leislerian party, and had the casting vote. This proceeding on the part of the Mayor created intense excitement, and threatened the peace of the city.

Lord Cornbury, a nephew of Queen Anne, who had just ascended the throne, was appointed to succeed Lord Bellomont. Bayard, who had labored to secure the conviction and execution of Leisler and Milburne, having prepared the act under which they were executed, upon hearing of the appointment of Cornbury, transmitted papers to him and to Parliament, strongly condemning the Leislerians and abusing Nanfan and his administration. Nanfan, learning of the action of Bayard, immediately arrested him and his associate, John Hutchins, for treasonable acts in vilifying the administration. Bayard had the misfortune to be tried under the same act which he had prepared for the benefit of Leisler. The act provided " that any person who should endeavor by any manner or way, or upon any pretense, by force of arms or otherwise, to disturb the peace, good, and quiet, of the province, should be esteemed rebels and traitors, and should incur the pains and penalties which the laws of England had provided for such offenses."

Bayard had enforced this law without semblance of pity, but with rancor and hatred in his heart toward Leisler and Milburne. His own hour had come! As he had meted out to others, so he himself was to receive. He could expect no clemency. Bayard was indicted for treason and rebellion, for inciting the soldiers in the fort against the constituted authorities, and for inducing his friends to sign libelous petitions and addresses. Great exertions were made to secure his acquittal, without avail. He was tried, found guilty of the offense, and sentenced to death. Hutchins met with a similar fate. Leisler was not allowed opportunity to appeal for a reprieve, but Bayard and Hutchins received more merciful treatment. Governor Nanfan gave them a reprieve until the matter could be presented to the King and his wishes ascertained. In the mean time Lord Cornbury arrived, and exercised executive clemency by their release. Bayard was again taken in favor by Cornbury, who denounced the Leislerians and identified himself with the party in opposition. The judge who passed sentence on Bayard was obliged to leave the country, having by his conduct incurred the displeasure of the Governor and Council.

Cornbury's administration was intolerant toward every religious and educational advancement. He embraced every opportunity which presented itself to rob and plunder the treasury, and enrich himself thereby. Although his opportunities for enrichment were great, yet he possessed no capacity for saving that which he secured. His recklessness and licentiousness caused him to become deeply involved in debt, and rendered him unpopular with the people; public sentiment was, indeed, strongly against him. This fact, in connection with his general and reckless disobedience of orders, caused his recall in 1708. His creditors, who had looked upon his advancement to the position of Governor as a golden opportunity to secure their claims, feeling keenly the disappointment of not receiving their just dues, and becoming greatly incensed against him, on his return to England had him arrested and cast into prison, where he remained until the death of his father, whom he succeeded in the peerage.

The condition of the negro slave at this time was one of degradation. The negro's privileges were circumscribed, and strict laws were enforced concerning his habits and movements. In order to pass the gates the slaves were obliged to obtain permission of their masters, and were not allowed to meet together. They could not own property, and there were no means provided whereby they could obtain their freedom. If an owner desired to give his slave his freedom, he was liable to pay a heavy fine for transgressing the law. These burdens daily increased. The traffic in slaves became more and more popular as a business.

In order to supply the demand, a public market for slaves was opened in New York in 1711. It was located at the foot of Wall Street, and it was the practice to bring all the slaves who were to be sold or hired to this market, where they could be inspected as so many cattle by parties desiring to bid. So strict were the ordinances passed concerning negroes that they were not allowed to appear in the streets at night unless they had a lighted lantern. All who violated this regulation were committed to jail, and kept in confinement until a fine of eight shillings was paid. The master or owner of the slave on paying this fine enjoyed the privilege of requiring the authorities to give the offending slave thirty-nine lashes at the public whipping-post. It was not unnatural that these regulations should breed among the negroes at times a spirit of rebellion. They committed many murders in retaliation for injuries received.

At Newtown, in 1707, an entire family was murdered by the slaves. On being apprehended, the murderers acknowledged their offense, and gave as a reason for committing the crime that they had been prevented from going out on Sunday. The punishment instituted for the murderous acts of slaves was calculated to fill them with fear and dread. They were even "tied to stakes and burned alive, broken on wheels, or suspended to the limbs of trees and left to perish." Seldom in the world's history has so much inhumanity been manifested towards slaves as in the early days of the colonies.

In 1706, Lord Cornbury issued the following proclamation to the justices of the peace in Kings County: —

By his Excellency, Edward, Lord Viscount Cornbury, Captain General and Governor in Chief of the provinces of New York and New Jersey, and the territories depending thereon in America, and Vice Admiral of the same, etc.: Whereas, I am informed that several negroes in Kings County have assembled themselves in a riotous manner, which if not prevented may prove of ill consequence; you and every one of you are therefore hereby required and commanded to take all proper methods for seizing and apprehending all such negroes in the said county, as shall be found to be assembled in such manner as aforesaid, or have run away or absconded from their masters or owners, whereby there may be reason to suspect them of ill practices or designs, and to secure them in safe custody, that their crimes and actions may be inquired into; and if any of them refuse to submit themselves, then to fire on them, kill, or destroy them, if they cannot otherwise be taken; and for so doing this shall be your sufficient warrant. Given under my hand at Fort Anne, in New York, the 22d day of July, 1706.

CORNBURY.

Furman, in his "Antiquities," refers to the condition of slaves on Long Island, and bears testimony that as a general rule they were peaceable and well behaved. He says that they were much attached to the families to which they belonged. Many now living can bear testimony to this fact. When slavery was abolished in New York it was provided that all who had reached a certain age should remain with their owners and be provided during life with proper support and care. The writer can now call to mind many old negroes who never obtained their freedom. They loved to talk of "massa" and the boys. They considered themselves a part of the family, and often idolized their owners. The master had in them true, warm friends, ever ready to fight his battles and take his part.

The aged negroes loved to sit in the chimney corner and tell to the children the history of the family. They would narrate in glowing language the incidents of the past, and always had eager listeners. They were rarely sold or separated from the family. When a son or daughter was married, a slave became a portion of the dowry or outfit. At times when estates were divided it became necessary to dispose of them. Furman says "that in an inventory taken on the 16th of December, 1719, in Kings County, of the estate of a deceased person, a negro wench and child were valued at £60, while five milk cows, five calves, three young bulls, and two heifers were collectively valued at £20."

New York was visited during the time of Lord Cornbury with that terrible scourge of the human race, yellow fever. It was brought from St. Thomas and spread rapidly. Physicians seemed powerless to prevent its ravages.

It was an epidemic long remembered and dreaded by the citizens of New York. All who could get away fled either to Jersey or Long Island. Lord Cornbury, with his retinue, took up his residence in Jamaica, Long Island. In order to afford suitable accommodations for so high a dignitary as the Governor, the Presbyterian minister of the village cheerfully gave up his parsonage to his use, removing himself to a smaller and less pretentious house.

In return for this act of kindness, Cornbury was guilty of a very contemptible trick toward the Presbyterian minister and church. The Governor was an uncompromising supporter of the Established Church of England, and was ready at all times to advance her interests. The Presbyterian church of Jamaica was strong and prosperous. Its popularity made the few Episcopalians in the village jealous and anxious to secure the property. The presence of Cornbury induced them to take possession of the building on a Sunday afternoon between services. This act resulted in violence between the parties, each of which claimed title. The pews were torn out, and the turmoil was only quelled by the appearance of the Governor, who decided that the Episcopalians were entitled to possession.

BROOKLYN CHURCH AND DUFFIELD HOUSE, 1776

A law suit followed, and the Episcopalians kept possession until 1728. The sheriff also seized the parsonage and land, and leased it for the benefit of the Episcopal Church. Cornbury, having been kindly treated by the minister, rewarded the act of courtesy by surrendering the house into the hands of the Episcopal rector, who took possession and occupied the house when Cornbury returned to New York.

Cornbury was succeeded in 1710 by Robert Hunter, who was a man of fine abilities, good character, possessed of excellent business qualities, and of a varied experience. He was one who in our day would pass for a very good Yankee. He was born of humble Scotch parents, who had not the means to supply him with an education. He was in a great measure a "self-made" man. When very young he was apprenticed to an apothecary. This employment not suiting his taste, he ran away and enlisted in the army as a private. Possessing honesty and perseverance, and withal having a desire to please his superior officers, he soon gained their affection and good will, and was placed in the line of promotion. His manliness gained him friends everywhere, and in a short time the poor Scotch lad rose to the rank of a brigadier general. He was now thrown into the society of the cultivated and refined.

Hunter married an heiress, through whose instrumentality he was appointed Lieutenant-Governor of Virginia. He started for his new field of labor in 1707, was captured by a French cruiser and taken back to Europe as a prisoner. He was exchanged after having been a prisoner only a short time. What at first seemed to be a hardship in his case proved a blessing, and the precursor of higher honors. Upon being released the Queen removed the gall from the bitterness he had endured by bestowing upon him the position of governor of the provinces of New York and New Jersey.

Hunter considered it a paramount duty on his part to enforce the requirements of the Crown. In acting in accordance with their wishes he was compelled to oppose every manifestation of republican feeling on the part of the people, and to ally himself with the aristocratic party. He chose his councillors from this party, but was careful to select men of intelligence and power. Among his first advisers might be mentioned Gerardus Beekman, Rip Van Dam, an honest and successful Dutch merchant; Killian Van Rensselaer, whose family were patroons on the Hudson. The Huguenots were represented in his Cabinet by John Barbarie and Frederic Philipse. Hunter was deeply interested in the Huguenot element of the population.

Governor Hunter had a fixed desire to acquire additional territory for his Queen. He projected an expedition to conquer Canada, and used his influence to induce New England to join in the enterprise. This was in 1711. It was a measure which met with hearty acquiescence in New York. The attention of the Assembly was brought to the subject, and at once an appropriation of ten thousand pounds was made to defray the necessary expenses. The Assembly issued bills of credit, and they may be said to be the beginnings of paper money in our country, as such notes had never before been used in the colony.

In 1712, after the failure of the expedition for conquest, rumors of an intended negro rebellion were heard on every side. It was noticed that the movements of the slaves were mysterious, and the general opinion was that the slaves intended to cause a riot; and a natural alarm spread through the communities on Manhattan Island and on the Brooklyn side of the river. These fears were not unfounded.

The smouldering fire burst out into a flame. Property was destroyed, one house was burned, and several white men were killed. It was resolved to make a general arrest of the negroes. Nineteen were taken, tried, and executed for their connection with the disturbance.

In 1713, the war between England and France terminated by the treaty of Utrecht, which put an end to the effort to conquer Canada.

Hunter's health failing, in 1719, after a term of nine years, he was obliged to seek a change of climate, and returned to England, leaving the administration of affairs in the hands of his trusty friend, Peter Schuyler. He bade adieu to New York in July, 1719, bearing with him the good wishes of the people.

Schuyler's official career was short, lasting but one year. His long residence and connection with public matters proved of service to himself and the people he governed, and rendered his short administration eminently successful. He exercised great influence with the Indians, having ever shown himself to be their friend and protector, and having on many occasions interceded with them, and thereby saved the settlement from invasion and destruction. One of his principal and most worthy acts was the restoration of friendship between the whites and Iroquois Indians, which gave him deserved popularity.

The next governor was William Burnet, a son of the celebrated Bishop Burnet. He arrived on the 17th of September, 1720, immediately assumed control and entered upon his duties as governor of the combined provinces of New York and New Jersey. He was a man of education and ability, and above all things else was thoroughly honest. He readily saw that the wisdom and prudence of Hunter had been beneficial to the colony, and he resolved to follow the same course his predecessor had pursued. One of his first acts was to continue the Assembly which had been convened by Hunter, and he kept it in existence for eleven years. The Assembly manifested its confidence and gratification by voting him a revenue for the succeeding five years.

It was soon after the opening of Burnet's administration that the people of Brooklyn and Kings County began to give signs of annoyance and agitation over encroachments made by private owners upon the king's highway leading from the ferry, and now represented by Fulton Street. This highway, as we have seen, had been laid out in 1704, by the duly constituted commissioners, and it was provided "that it was to be ffour rod wide and to continue forever."

In April, 1721, the General Sessions of the Peace for Kings County held its term, and, after a due consideration of the question, indictments for encroaching on the "common highway of the King leading from the ferry to the church," were found against John Rapalje, Hans Bergen, and others. It appears very singular that these indictments were obtained at the instance and upon the complaint of two of the indicted parties.

The complaint on which this indictment was obtained was as follows: —

Flatbush, April 19, 1721. John Rapalje and Hans Bergen of the fferry desires of the Grand Jury that the Commissioners own being should be presented for not doing there duty in laying the King's highway according to ye law, being the King's highway is too narrow from the ferry to one Nicolus Cowenhoven living at Brooklyn, and if all our neighbours will make ye road according to law, then ye said John Rapalje and Hans Bergen is willing to do the same as aforesaid, being they are not willing to suffer more than their neighbors. As witness our hands the day and year first above written. JAN RAPALJE.
HANS BERGEN.

These men were governed by a desire that all should fare alike, demanding that the law should be enforced without fear, favor, or partiality.

Some of the persons indicted, in connection with others who felt aggrieved and feared that they also might be placed in a similar unpleasant position, applied to the Colonial Legislature, and secured the passage of a law on the 27th of July, 1721, "to continue the common road or King's highway from the ferry toward the Town of Breuckland, on the Island of Nassau, in the Province of New York." The preamble was as follows: " Whereas, Several of the inhabitants on the ferry on the Island of Nassau, by their petition, preferred to the General Assembly, by setting forth that they have been molested by persecutions, occasioned by the contrivance and instigations of ill and disaffected persons, to the neighborhood, who would encroach upon the buildings and fences that have been made many years, alledging the road was not wide enough, to the great damage of several of the old inhabitants, on the said ferry, the said road as it now is, has been so for sixty years past without any complaint either of the inhabitants or travellers."

The remaining sections of the law established the road "forever," as it then existed, from the ferry upward to the town of Breuckland, as far as the swinging gate of John Rapalje, just above the property belonging to James Harding. The unwillingness of the early settlers to part with their land, when land was so cheap, accounts in a great measure for our present narrow and crooked street. These early settlers, in their opposition to the widening of the street, might have desired to preserve some favorite fruit or shade tree. It has been given as a reason why Broadway, New York, makes a turn or diverges at Grace Church, that a Dutchman had a favorite cherry tree on the line of the thoroughfare as proposed, and, if the street was continued in a direct line, the tree would have felt the woodman's axe.

Another provision of this enactment was the privilege it gave that, if a majority of the inhabitants of the town should "adjudge that part of the road near to the ferry to be too narrow and inconvenient," they could take proceedings to have it widened. In order to secure this improvement, "they might cause the sheriff to summon a jury of twelve men to appraise the value of land to be taken, and the amount of value so ascertained should be levied upon the towne, and collected and paid to the owners of the land so appropriated to street purpose."

This provision of the law was never enforced. The people seemed to rest content with their narrow, winding, crooked lane, which in those days resembled a cow-path. The "swinging gate" referred to, is said to have been located on the rise of the hill at or near the junction of Sands and Fulton streets.

The commissioners of highways laid out another important highway or road on the 28th of March, 1704. It led to the public landing place at the mills of Nehemiah Denton at Gowanus. The record of this road is as follows: —

"One common highway to Gowanus Mill, to begin from the northeast corner of Leffert Peterses ffence, and soe along the road westerly as it is now in use, to the lane yt parts the lands of Hendrick Vechte, and Abraham Brower and Nicholas Brower, and soe all along said lane, as it is now in ffence to the house of Jurian Collier, and from thence all along the roade, now in use to the said Gowanus Mill, being in all four rod wide to the said lane, and that there be a convenient landing place for all persons whatsoever, to begin ffrom said southermost side of said Gowanus Mill house, and ffrom said house to run ffour rod to the southward, for the transportation of goods, and the commodious passage of travellers; and that said highway to the said Gowanus Mill ffrom said house of said Jurian Collier, shall be but two rod only, and where it is now in use said common highway to be and continue forever; and ffurther that the ffence and gate that now stands upon the entrance into said mill neck, shall soe remain and be alwayes kept soe enclosed with a ffence and hanging gate; and the way to said mill to be thorou that gate only, and to be alwayes shutt or put to, by all persons that passes thorou."

In 1709 another road[1] and landing place had been laid out at or near the mill of John C. Friecke.

Brooklyn's political fortunes were at this period so intimately connected with those of New York city that the political history of one is, in general, the political history of the other; yet Brooklyn and Kings County held suffi-

[1] The description of this road in the records is as follows: "One common highway to begin ffrom the house of Jurian Collier to the new mill of Nicholas Brower, now sett upon Gowanus Mill neck soe called, as the way is now in use, along said neck to said mill to be of two rods wide, and that there shall be a landing place by said mill in the most convenient place ffor the transportation of goods, and the commodious passing of travellers; and said highway and landing place to be, remaine and continue forever."

ciently aloof to justify the omission of any particular chronicle of the administration of Burnet and its quarrels with the French, or the circumstances attending the Governor's transfer to Massachusetts by George II.

The next Governor, John Montgomerie, was instructed to continue the policy of Hunter, but he had not the firmness to do so.

The principal event in Montgomerie's administration, and one which is held in lasting remembrance in New York, was the grant of an amended charter to the city in 1730. This charter, as well as the Dongan charter, of which it was an amendment, is one which has always been of interest to Brooklyn, as it claimed to fix the limits of the city of New York. The limits thus embraced in the charter extended to low-water mark on the Long Island shore.[1]

On the death of Montgomerie, in 1731, the Governorship passed temporarily to Rip Van Dam, senior member of the Council, in whose accession the Dutch elements in New York and Kings County rejoiced greatly.

Colonel William Crosby, who became Governor in 1732, was guilty of infamous tyrannies and usurpations, as in the Van Dam trial, and

[1] For comment on Brooklyn's claims, see appendix.

later in the persecution of John Peter Zenger, publisher of the "Weekly Journal," a newspaper started in opposition to the administration "Gazette" and to voice the popular opposition.

Under Crosby's instigation the Council promulgated an order directing that the papers containing the obnoxious articles should be burnt by the hangman at the pillory. When this order was presented to the Quarter Sessions the Aldermen protested strongly against it, and the court thereupon refused to allow it to be entered on the records. The Recorder, Francis Harrison, was the only one who attempted to defend it, and he based its regularity upon former English precedents. The court also refused to allow the hangman to execute the order, and it was carried into effect by a negro slave, hired for the purpose. The negro did his work in the presence of the Recorder and other partisans of the government. The magistrates, with great and commendable unanimity, refused to attend, and evidently considered that the whole proceeding was but on a par with the former actions of the adherents of the Crown.

The burning of the papers did not satisfy the aristocratic party. They desired to be avenged, and, thirsting for a victim, shortly after caused the arrest of Zenger on the charge that he had been guilty of publishing treasonable and seditious libels against the Government and her representatives. He was imprisoned on this complaint, and, while in jail awaiting the action of the grand jury, was treated in a cruel and inhuman manner by his jailers. The ordinary courtesies usually granted to unconvicted men were denied him. He was even refused the use of pen, ink, and paper. The jail of the city at that time was in the City Hall, in Wall Street. Here Zenger was imprisoned.

Application was made by his friends to have him submitted to bail, and for the purpose of having the amount fixed, he was brought before the court on a writ of *habeas corpus*. The court required him to give bail in the sum of £400, with two additional sureties in the sum of £200 each. This was virtually a denial of bail, as he could not procure the requisite amount. In his endeavor to get his bail reduced, he swore that he was not worth, exclusive of his trade tools, the sum of £40. On this affidavit he was remanded to his place of confinement.

The trial of Zenger occasioned great excitement on both sides of the East River. The acquittal brought immense enthusiasm and lavish honors on Andrew Hamilton, who brilliantly defended the popular publisher.

In the Assembly called in 1737, under Governor Clarke, Kings County was represented by Samuel Garretson, Abraham Lott, and Johannis Lott.

Brooklyn's population in 1738 was 721. In the same year the population of the other settlements was as follows: Flatbush, 540; Bushwick, 302; New Utrecht, 282; Flatlands, 268; Gravesend, 235.

The breaking out of virulent smallpox in New York brought the Assembly of 1745-46 to Brooklyn, a matter of momentous interest to the little hamlet. The house of "Widow Sickle" was honored by the Assembly as a place of meeting, and its great room was so occupied for several months.

During Governor Clinton's term smallpox appeared a second time in New York (in 1752), and the Colonial Assembly again sought quarters in Brooklyn in which to hold their deliberations. The Legislature chose a house on Fulton Street near Nassau. It was at this important session that, on the 4th of June, 1752, the Colonial Commissioners canceled bills of credit, issued by the Colony of New York, amounting to the sum of £3,602 18s. 3d. The Assembly manifested no little acrimony toward the Governor and displayed a growing feeling of independence.

This independence of the representatives of the people appeared with increasing frequency, and signs of it so preyed upon gloomy Sir Danvers Osborne, who succeeded Clinton, that he hanged himself with a handkerchief in his garden, shortly after his inauguration, leaving Lieutenant-Governor DeLancey[1] to assume control of the government.

[1] To DeLancey belongs the honor of signing the charter of Columbia College in New York, first known as Kings College, an institution in which Brooklynites have always taken a deep interest. Among her graduates from Brooklyn may be mentioned the ex-mayor, ex-senator, and ex-minister to the Hague, Henry C. Murphy, who graduated in 1830. The Hon. Alexander McCue, of the City Court, was the valedictorian of the class of 1845. Ex-supervisor William J. Osborne, Henry C. Murphy, Jr., George I. Murphy, Richard M. De Mille, John Lockwood, of Lockwood's Academy; George W. Collard, the erudite professor of languages in the Polytechnic; Stewart L. Woodford, and Edgar M. Cullen all graduated from Columbia. Beside these might be mentioned John L. Lefferts, Van Brunt Wyckoff, ex-mayor Edward Copeland, who graduated in 1809; the late Samuel E. Johnson, ex-county judge, who graduated in 1834, and the late Rev. Stephen H. Meeker, who for fifty years was pastor of the old Bushwick Church. Among the clergy who enjoyed her academic shades might be mentioned the late Rev. Dr. Dwight, who for many years was pastor of the Joralemon Street Dutch Church; the Right Rev. Henry Ustick Onderdonk, at one time rector of St. Ann's Church and subsequently bishop of Pennsylvania; Rev. Dr.

Meanwhile one phase of Long Island's relations to New York should not escape notice. The position of Long Island made it natural that New York should look to it as in a measure a bulwark against attack from the sea, and various governors displayed an interest in repairing those harbor fortifications which rested on the Island.

Governor Clarke addressed the Legislature, in 1741, in the following terms: " There is great reason to apprehend a speedy rupture with France; your situation ought therefore to awaken you to a speedy provision against that event, in fortifying the town in a better manner than it is at present by erecting batteries in proper places upon some of the wharves facing the harbor, others upon the side of the Hudson River adjoining the town, and one at Red Hook, upon Long Island, to

---

Samuel Roosevelt Johnson, formerly rector of St. John's Church; the Right Rev. Dr. George F. Seymour, formerly rector of St. John's Church and now bishop of Springfield. Of the legal profession who have graduated from her law school might be mentioned William H. Ingersoll, Edward B. Barnum, Henry Broadhead, Abel Crook, William Leggett Whiting, Philip L. Wilson, Henry S. Bellows, Merwin Rushmore, F. A. Ward, D. D. Terry, L. Bradford Prince, Daniel W. Northup, and a host of other well known members of the bar. Of the medical profession the number from Brooklyn is legion. — S. M. O.

We may now add to the roll a conspicuous name, that of ex-mayor Seth Low, now president of Columbia.

prevent the enemy from landing at Nutten Island."

Governor Clinton, on April 30, 1744, assured the Legislature in a special message that "it was absolutely necessary there should be a battery of six guns at Red Hook, on Nassau Island, which would effectually prevent the enemy's lying there, to bombard the city, or their landing any force or artillery on Nutten Island. In case of any such attack upon us, this battery might be easily supplied and maintained by the force of the country."

Of life on Long Island and throughout the Colony during the period immediately preceding the Revolution we find many interesting glimpses through the medium of newspapers of the time.

The "Weekly Post Boy" of June 18, 1753, contained an advertisement which was of interest to the citizens of Long Island: —

Notice is hereby given that the Ferry House from Long Island to Staten Island, commonly known by the name of the Upper Ferry, otherwise Stillwell's Ferry, is now kept by Nicholas Stillwell, who formerly occupy'd the same; he has two good Boats well accommodated for the safe Conveyance of Man or Horse across the Narrows. He also proposes to carry, if required, travellers either to Staten Island, Elizabethtown Point, Amboy, or New York, and that at the most reasonable terms. He continues to keep good entertainment for travellers. NICHOLAS STILLWELL.

John Lane advertised in the "Mercury" June 18, 1753, as follows: —

This is to inform the Publick that John Lane now keeps the ferry at Yellow Hook, 6 miles below New York ferry on Long Island, and has provided good boats, well fitted, with proper hands, and will be ready at all times (wind and weather permitting) to go to Smith's Ferry on Staten Island, with a single man only. There will be good entertainment at said house, where all gentlemen travellers and others may expect the best of usage, for themselves and horses, from their very humble servant, JOHN LANE.

N. B. Travellers are desired to observe in going from Flat Bush to said ferry to keep the mark'd trees on the right hand.

The Free and Accepted Masons are referred to by the "Mercury" as having observed in due form the anniversary of St. John. Its account of the proceedings is as follows: "Sunday the 24th ult., being the Anniversary of the Festival of St. John the Baptist, the Ancient and Right Worshipful Society of

Free and Accepted Masons, of this City, assembled at Spring Garden, the next Day, and being properly cloathed, made a regular Procession in due Form, to the Kings Arms Tavern in Broad Street, near the Long Bridge, where an elegant Entertainment was provided; and after drinking his Majesty's and several other loyal Healths, the Day was concluded in the most social manner, and to the entire satisfaction of all the Company."

The following peculiar advertisement appeared in the "Post Boy" in 1753: —

"By a person lately arrived in this Town, Painting upon Glass (commonly call'd burning upon Glass) is performed in a neat and curious Manner so as to never change its Colour; Perspective Views neatly colour'd for the Camera Obscura.

"N. B. Young gentlemen and ladies are instructed in either of the above, so as to be capable to perform it themselves in a little Time, at a reasonable Rate. By the same person, Land Surveyed, Designs for Buildings, Plans and Maps neatly drawn. Enquire at Mr. John Ditcher's Tallow Chandler and Soap Boiler in the Sloat."

It would appear that Bedloe's Island at that time was private property, and was considered by the owner to be very valuable. He advertised: —

"To be Let, Bedloe's Island, alias Love Island, together with the Dwelling House and Light House, being finely situated for a tavern where all kinds of Garden Stuff, Poultry, &c., may be easily raised for the shipping outward bound, and from where any Quantity of pickled Oysters may be transported; it abounds with English Rabbits."

The "New York Gazette" of July 23, 1753, made an announcement, of interest to Presbyterians, that —

"Inasmuch as it was yesterday the declared Intention of the Presbyterian Church in this City to make use of the Version of Psalms Known by the Name of Mr. Watt's in their publick Worship, this may serve to acquaint all concerned, that an Impression of these Psalms was done here in the year 1750, in order to supply two or three neighboring congregations, which are now almost all sold off, and a new Impression begun, which would have been finished as Leisure Time permitted; but as there is likely to be a small Demand quickly for them, the Impression will be now proceeded in immediately, and finished with all Dispatch; so that in a very few Weeks they will be ready. And all such Families of this City, as shall take three or more of them at once, shall at any time before the 1st of November next, have them at the wholesale price of 2s. per Book, and singly 2s. 4d., plain bound, and others who incline to have them neatly bound will have them at the Difference for the Binding. On Notification some time ago, that the new Version of Psalms by Tate and Brady was to be introduced into that Church, an Impression was immediately made of them, which fell upon the Printer's Hands; he presumes, therefore, that all such as occasioned his Damage in these, will prefer the Purchasing of these of him to any other. N. B. — The above Impression of Tate and Brady's Psalms is a pretty good one, and to be sold bound very cheap."

In these days the Scottish settlers kept alive the remembrance of home. Their quarterly meeting received the following notice: —

"The members of the Scots Society, in this City, are desired to take Notice, that their Quarterly Meeting is on Wednesday evening, the 1st of August next, at the House of Mr. Malcolm McEwen, near the City Hall."

On the 4th of June, 1753, we have seen that notice was given of the drawing of a lottery for the benefit of the Presbyterians. On the 23d of July following, notice was published that, " By a law passed the last sessions, a publick Lottery is directed for a further provision toward founding a College for the Advancement of Learning within this Colony, to consist of 5,000 tickets at Thirty shillings each, 1,094 of which are to be fortunate."

There was to be one prize of £500, and the lowest was £5. The notice continued: "Fifteen per cent. to be deducted from the Prizes: As such a laudable Design will greatly tend to the welfare and Reputation of this Colony, it is expected the Inhabitants will readily be excited to become Adventurers. Publick notice will be given of the precise Time of putting the Tickets in the Boxes, that such Adventurers as shall be minded to see the same done, may be present at the doing thereof. The Drawing to commence on the first Tuesday in November next, or sooner if full, at the City Hall of New York under the Inspection of the Corporation, who are impowered to appoint two or more of their Body to inspect all and every Transaction of the said Lottery; and two Justices of the Peace, or other reputable Freeholders of every county in this Colony, if they see cause to dispute the same at their next general Sessions of the Peace. Publick notice will be given fourteen Days before the Drawing. The managers are sworn faithfully to execute the Trust reposed in them, and have given Security for the faithful

Discharge of the same. Such as forge or counterfeit any Ticket or alter the Number, and are thereof convicted, are by the Acts to suffer Death as in the cases of Felony. The Prizes will be published in this paper, and the Money will be paid to the Possessors of the Benefit Tickets as soon as the Drawing is finished. Tickets are to be had at the Dwelling House of Messieurs Jacobus Roosevelt and Peter Van Burgh Livingston, who are appointed managers. The managers would acquaint the Publick, that upwards of one thousand Tickets are already engaged to the Hand in Hand and American Fire Companies in this City, to whom the Tickets are already delivered. The Prosperity of the Community greatly depending upon the regular Education of Youth, it is not doubted but that the Lottery will soon fill; Those therefore that Design to become Adventurers are desired speedily to apply for Tickets or they may be disappointed."

An advertisement announces the sale of "Joyce's great wound balsam," a "corrector for coughs and colds," and other things, at Edward Joyce's shop "near the Brooklyn ferry." Israel Horsfield offers "two negro men, one of which has served with a ship carpenter, and is a good caulker, and has lately served with a brewer and maltster, and is very handy." The widow Rapalje at the Brooklyn ferry was robbed, in 1768, of "a gold ring, seven silver spoons, one pair of gold sleeve-buttons, two Johannesses, two doubloons, two New York £5 bills, and about £40 in Jersey bills and dollars." A negro named Cæsar was the thief, and, being found guilty, he was executed.

In August, 1771, Ares Remsen, at the Wallabout, offered 20 shillings reward for a "negro man, Newport, Guinea-born, and branded on the breast with three letters." On Sunday, February 24, 1773, "the coldest day for more than half a century," the harbor and river were so full of ice "that many people walked over to Brooklyn and back again." By a notice in the "Mercury" of February 21, 1774, it appears that a ferry was established from Coenties Market, New York, to the landing-place of P. Livingston, Esq., and Henry Remsen, on Long Island, and another from Fly Market, and a third from Peck Slip "to the present ferry-house at Brooklyn." The Livingston landing was near the foot of the present Joralemon Street. "St. George's Ferry," as this was called, was operated for not more than two years.

Speaking of Brooklyn affairs " Rivington's Gazette " (March 31, 1774), says: " Many persons have been misled by an opinion that the church proposed to be erected by lottery, at Brooklyn, is to be under the ministry of the Rev. Mr. Bernard Page. It will be a truly orthodox church, strictly conformable to the doctrine and discipline of the Constitutional Church of England as by law established, and under the patronage of the Rev. Rector and Vestry of Trinity Church."

It was at Tower Hill, on the Heights, near St. George's Ferry, that a tavern was opened in May, 1774, and according to an advertisement, in August following, there was to be " a bull baited on Tower Hill, at three o'clock in the afternoon, every Thursday during the season."

Meanwhile the relations of the American colonists with Great Britain had begun to show more than a slight strain. George III. ascended the throne in 1760. In 1765 Grenville became the Prime Minister of England. Grenville held that England had a right to impose taxes and regulate the affairs of the colonies without consulting their wishes in the premises. As a result of his efforts in this direction, an act was passed providing for a tax on articles which had previously been entered free of duty. To enforce the same the powers and jurisdiction of the courts in admiralty were enlarged. These acts were looked upon by the colonists as tyrannical. At first, the people could not believe the report. When they came to realize the facts, their indignation knew no bounds. Meetings were held nightly, and the measures were denounced in severe terms as unjust and tyrannical. This feeling was not confined to the city of New York alone, but was manifest in all the settlements of the colony. Protests were prepared and freely signed against the proposed Stamp Act, and urging the immediate repeal of the Sugar Act, which had recently become a law.

The Assembly in its session in March, 1764, passed stringent resolutions in opposition to the invasion of their vested rights, and forwarded a forcible memorial to the ministry in opposition to the enforcement of the obnoxious acts. It should be borne in mind that the Assembly was composed of delegates or members from the twelve counties included in the province of New York, three of which counties were on Long Island.[1] The County of Kings

[1] Kings, Queens, and part of Suffolk.

was represented by Simon Boerum and Abraham Schenck. At this time Abraham Lott, Jr., of Kings County, was Clerk of the Assembly. The members from Kings County received seventy-five cents per diem, and were paid by their constituents, and the same sum per day for the time consumed in their journey to New York, also paid by their constituents. The language used in the remonstrance of the Assembly was bold and decided. It did not beg the question, but was spirited, severe, and just in its condemnation of the overt acts of Parliament. The Assembly and the citizens were destined to be severely punished for the bravery they displayed in the defense of their rights. The action of the Assembly resulted in the total suspension of legislative prerogatives, and deprived the people of their representation in the government of the colony. The neighboring colonies also sent petitions on the subject to Parliament. These were received because they were couched in feebler language, and after consideration were rejected. To the credit of New York it must be said that she presented her objections in a bold and fearless manner. Her Assembly spoke in trumpet tones that gave no uncertain sound. The import and meaning of her protest could not be misunderstood, and showed her people to possess something of Roman fortitude and firmness. Had the sister colonies at the outset manifested the same vigorous spirit as was displayed by the descendants of the defenders of Leyden, Parliament would not have dared to pass the reprehensible acts. The inhabitants of New Amsterdam kindled the fire which was to produce a revolutionary flame of glory. It was well for the country that the citizens of New York so early manifested patriotic feeling, and the spirit which was inwrought in them furnished the leaven which was destined to infuse itself into the New England and other colonies, and to ultimately bear fruit in independence.

In March, 1765, Parliament set further torch to the colonial spirit by passing the celebrated Stamp Act. When the time came for the enforcement of this act the country gave unmistakable signs of its resentment, and New York was conspicuously rebellious in mood.

At last the eyes of Parliament were opened. They saw that it was useless to attempt to force the colonists to submit to the outrageous measure, and reluctantly repealed the act on February 20, 1766. The news of the repeal was received in New York May 20, 1766, — three months after the action of Parliament. Its reception filled the community with joy. The bells of the city rang forth joyful peals of praise and thanksgiving. In honor of the event, bonfires were kindled in prominent places, and a public dinner was given by the corporation. Again, on June 4, 1766, being the anniversary of the King's birthday, another celebration was had by the patriots on the commons, near where the City Hall now stands. A barbecue was held, whereat roast ox, beer, and punch were provided in sufficient quantities to supply the wants of all. The greatest enthusiasm prevailed. A liberty pole was erected, amid the cheers of the people, which bore the inscription, " The King, Pitt, and Liberty." Every citizen felt proud that he had asserted his manhood, and had secured a recognition of his rights. This standard of liberty was destined to have an eventful history and to figure conspicuously at a later day.

During these trying times the Kings County officials were: Jeremiah Vanderbilt, Sheriff, who held office from 1763 to 1766; Samuel Garritson, Common Pleas Judge, who served in that capacity from 1749 to 1767; Abraham Lott, Jr., of Kings County, who was Clerk of the Assembly from 1751 to 1767; William Nicoll, of Suffolk County, who was Speaker of the Assembly, holding that office from 1761 to 1768. Kings County was represented in the Assembly by the following sterling men: —

Abraham Lott, from 1737 to 1750.

D. Vanderveer, from 1750 to 1759.

Abraham Schenck, from 1759 to 1768.

Simon Boerum, from 1761 to 1775.

Simon Boerum was also Clerk of Kings County from 1750 to 1775.

Governor Moore, having failed to control the Assembly, manifested his spite toward that body by formally dissolving them on the 11th of February, 1768, and directing a new election for members. His instructions were to secure the return of more pliable men than those composing the previous legislature. The people were not subservient to dictation, and, daring to maintain their principles, took good care to assert their manhood by electing men of firmness and decision.

In the new body Kings County was represented by Simon Boerum, John Rapalje, and Abraham Schenck. Queens County sent Daniel Kissam and Zebulon Seaman. Suffolk County elected Eleazor Miller and William Nicoll, second. Of these members so returned, all but John Rapalje were members of the recently dissolved Assembly. It may be supposed that such material would not readily submit to the exactions of the Crown. Philip Livingston, of New York, was chosen Speaker.

The new Assembly met in October, 1768, and at once proclaimed its independence and its contempt for royal dictation by opening a correspondence with the Assembly of Massachusetts. This was a direct and open violation of the commands which had been issued by his Majesty the King, which was that the colony should hold no correspondence with other provinces. A circular had been sent to the Assembly in New York from Massachusetts, in which the aid and assistance of New York was earnestly besought for coöperation in securing the removal of grievances which were common to all the colonies.

In the next Assembly the tone was so different as to excite the resentment of the patriots. Shortly afterward the soldiery and the people came into collision in trifling but significant ways. The so-called battle of Golden Hill was prophetic of the approaching revolution.

When Dunmore apprised the English government of the events which had taken place, he was careful to attribute them to party violence, encouraged by factious opposition to the Crown and the Established Church of England. He endeavored to make it appear that the contentions arose from the objections of the popular leaders to the enforcement of the laws passed by Parliament. Judging from the tenor of his report, one would be led to suppose that the soldiers were actuated solely by a desire to maintain and uphold the dignity of the government. They were specially commended for their exertions in subduing the rebellion.

Lord Dunmore, after a brief term in office, was succeeded in the office of Governor by William Tryon.

The "tea party" of April 23, 1774, illustrated the temper of the people. Other incidents of a less picturesque kind indicated not less clearly the determination to shake off the yoke of foreign control.

The General Assembly of New York, having at the time of its adjournment refused to comply with the recommendation of the Colonial Congress to elect delegates to attend another meeting of that body, to be held in the city of Philadelphia, May 10, 1775, a call was issued by the Committee of Sixty, in March, addressed

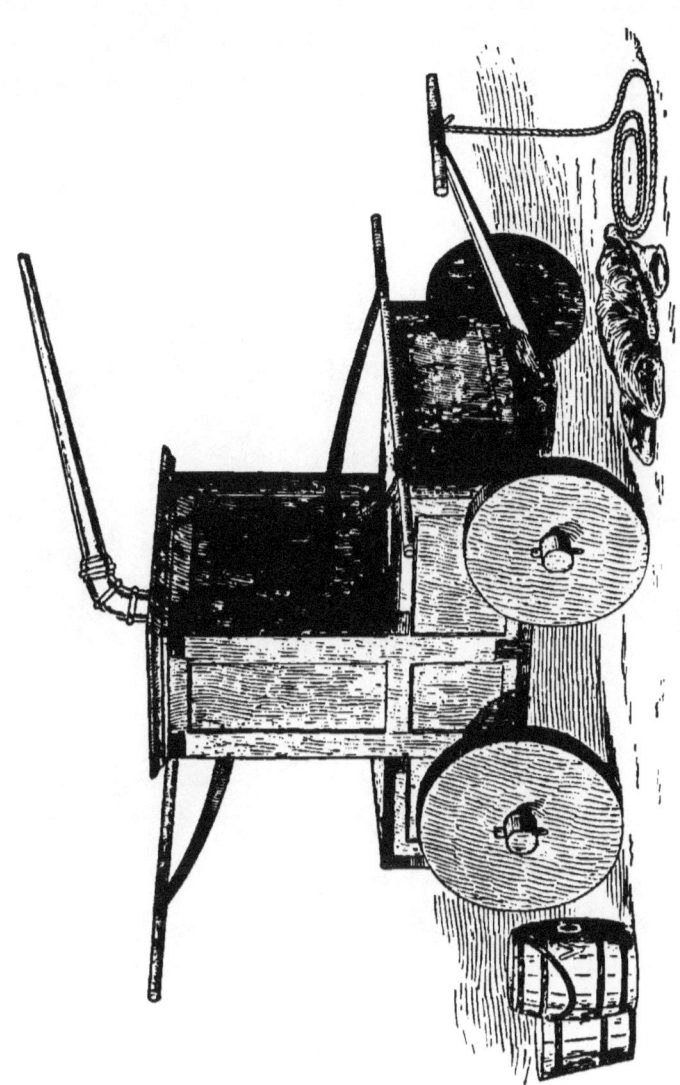

FIRST FIRE ENGINE USED IN BROOKLYN
Built in 1785

to the several counties throughout the colony, directing them to elect deputies to a provincial convention, to be held in the city of New York, on the 20th of April, for the purpose of choosing delegates to represent the colony in the Continental Congress. This convention, on the day appointed, met at the Exchange, in New York. Philip Livingston, one of the Committee of Sixty, was chosen president. Livingston, at this time, owned a very large tract of land in the neighborhood of Hicks and Joralemon streets, on which he had erected a handsome residence. In that body Kings County was represented by Simon Boerum, Denys Denice, Theodorus Polhemus, Richard Stillwell, and J. Vanderbilt. All of these men were well known, and enjoyed the confidence of their constituents.

At a meeting held on the 5th of May, a committee of one hundred of the first and foremost citizens of New York and Kings County was chosen to administer affairs during the political crisis. This committee was composed of such men as John Jay, the brave Welshman Francis Lewis, whose bold signature was appended to the Declaration of Independence, and who for many years resided and owned property in Brooklyn; Philip Livingston, the fearless; James Duane and John Alsop, who were members of the Colonial Congress of September, 1774, which met in Philadelphia; William Walton, whose house in Pearl Street was rendered famous as an ancient landmark; Augustus Van Horne, a stalwart Dutchman; Abraham Duryea, Samuel Verplanck, Abraham Brasher, Leonard Lispenard, Nicholas Hoffman, Lewis Pintard, Nicholas Bogart, Isaac Roosevelt, Gabriel H. Ludlow, Abraham Brinkerhoff, Henry Remsen, Benjamin Kissam, Jacob Lefferts, James Beekman, John Berrien, John Lamb, the daring and intrepid Richard Sharp, Jacob Van Voorhis, Comfort Sands, who afterward lived in Brooklyn; Peter Goelet, and James Desbrosses.

Just previous to the assembling of the Provincial Congress in New York, a general town meeting was held in Brooklyn. The official record of that meeting is as follows:—

At a general town meeting, regularly warned at Brooklyn, May 20, '75, the magistrates and freeholders met and voted Jer. Remsen, Esq., into the chair, and Leffert Lefferts, Esq., clerk.

Taking into our serious consideration the expediency and propriety of concurring with the freeholders and freemen of the City and County of New York, and the other colonies, townships and precincts within this province, for holding a Provincial Congress to advise, consult, watch over and defend, at this very alarming crisis, all our civil and religious rights, liberties and privileges, according to their collective prudence:

After duly considering the unjust plunder and inhuman carnage committed on the property and persons of our brethren in the Massachusetts colony, who, with the other New England colonies, are now deemed by the mother country to be in a state of actual rebellion, by which declaration England hath put it beyond her own power to treat with New England, or to propose or receive any terms of reconciliation until those colonies shall submit as a conquered country — the first effort to effect which was by military and naval force; the next attempt is, to bring a famine among them by depriving them both of their natural and acquired right of fishing. Further, contemplating the very unhappy situation to which the powers at home, by oppressive measures, have driven all the other provinces, we have all evils in their power to fear, as they have already declared all the provinces aiders and abettors of rebellion; therefore, first,

Resolved, That Henry Williams and Jer. Remsen, Esq., be now elected deputies for this township, to meet, May 22, with other deputies in Provincial Convention in New York, and there to consider, determine and do, all prudential and necessary business. Second,

Resolved, That we, confiding in the wisdom and equity of said convention, do agree to observe all warrantable acts, associations and orders, as said Congress shall direct.

Signed, by order of the town meeting.

LEFFERT LEFFERTS, Clerk.

Lieutenant-Governor Colden, who occupied the post of Governor during Tryon's absence in England, died in September, 1776, at his home at Spring Hill, Flushing, Long Island, aged 88 years.

CHAPTER VIII

KINGS COUNTY DURING THE REVOLUTION

1775-1783

Kings County at the Opening of the Revolution. Participation in Events leading to the Crisis. Military Officers. Long Island Tories. The Continental and Provincial Congresses. Fortifying. Declaration of Independence. General Greene on Long Island. Draft in Kings County. Landing of the British at Gravesend. The Battle of Brooklyn. The Night Retreat. British Occupation of the County. Temptations to Disloyalty toward the American Cause, and Action of the People under British Pressure. The County in Congress. Losses in the Battle. Incidents. Prisoners billeted on the Inhabitants of Kings County. Long Island Refugees. Conspicuous Figures of the Period. Peace.

THE position of Kings County, while actually close to the rapidly growing city on Manhattan Island, was relatively so much aloof in many of its interests from that storm centre of colonial activity in the middle colonies, that it was natural, perhaps, that there should be less enthusiasm over the independent cause than in New York itself, or than in certain other regions less sequestered geographically and by local condition.

But the quiet Dutch towns, if slow to anger under British rule, nevertheless acquired a definite patriotic energy as time advanced, in spite of peculiarly discouraging conditions introduced by British occupations. There may have been the appearance of lethargy, but Kings County's quietude in the face of excitement elsewhere did not mean a want of sympathy, but resulted from a special strain of suppression. "Many fowling-pieces," writes Stiles, "were cut down and fitted with bayonets, and those who had two guns loaned to those who had none."[1] The MS. of General Jeremiah Johnson, whose name is indelibly associated with the history of the Wallabout, tells us that Elijah Freeman Payne, the teacher of the Wallabout School, left his pupils to join the American forces at Boston.[2] The incident was typical.

Kings County watched, and also, as we have seen, participated in the events which led up to the crisis of active war.

When movements on the part of the British troops led the Continental Congress to consider the raising of men for common defense, the quota of the colony of New York was

[1] *History of the City of Brooklyn*, vol. i. p. 243.
[2] The school remained closed until 1777.

fixed at 3000, which number the Continental Congress directed them to raise. In obedience to this direction four regiments were raised, the Provincial Congress placing them under the command of Colonels Alexander McDougall, Gozen Van Schaick, James Clinton, and Holmes. The veteran Lamb received an appointment to command a company of artillery.

In Brooklyn an association was formed for mutual protection, and meetings were held weekly for the purpose of drilling, under the supervision of competent officers. Enthusiasm began to manifest itself. Every gun and bayonet was brought into requisition, and put in order and burnished for the coming fray. The meetings for drilling and instruction in the manual of arms, which were held at the Wallabout and other parts of Brooklyn, created much interest among the young men who opposed the Tory party, and prepared them for the service which they were soon after called upon to render.

In March, 1776, the following Brooklyn officers had taken commissions: — Half of Brooklyn: Barent Johnson, captain; Barent Lefferts, first lieutenant; Jost Debevoise, second lieutenant; Martin Schenck, ensign. Half of

Brooklyn: Fer'd Suydam, captain; John T. Bergen, first lieutenant; William Brower, second lieutenant; Jacob Stellenwerth, ensign. Kings County was further represented by Rutgert Van Brunt, colonel; Nich. Cowenhoven, lieutenant-colonel; Johannes Titus, first major; John Vanderbilt, second major; Geo. Carpenter, adjutant.[1]

The names of the military officers of this period were and have remained familiar in the history of Brooklyn. The Johnson estate was in the present seventh and nineteenth wards, being in the neighborhood of Kent Avenue, Hewes Street, and Bedford Avenue, a narrow strip also extending along Graham Street to Myrtle Avenue. The Lefferts property was in Flatbush and Bedford. The Schenck farm was situated on the site of the Wallabout Bay, and a portion of it is now occupied as the site of the United States Marine Hospital. The Suydam tract was situated in what was then known as Bushwick, and the Debevoise estate was also in the same section of the city. The Cowenhoven property was situated in what is now the heart of the city. The old house stood in a hollow near where the Atlantic

---

[1] Onderdonk, *Kings County*, p. 120.

avenue railroad depot now stands. It was an old-fashioned Dutch house, whose massive beams and quaint mantelpieces attracted considerable attention some twenty years ago when it was taken down. The history of this mansion and its occupants would form a very interesting chapter in the history of Brooklyn. The Bergen property was situated at Gowanus. The Vanderbilt farm was in the twentieth ward, between Clermont Avenue and Hamilton Street.

In consequence of the requisition made for troops, the colony of New York presented the appearance of military activity. Steps were taken to erect fortifications. The colony at this time had two governments, each of which was antagonistic to the other, and each one proclaimed the acts and resolutions of the other void and of no effect. Tryon represented the Crown as colonial governor, and the brave General Nathaniel Woodhull, of Long Island, as president *pro tem.* of the Provincial Congress, also acted as governor, and was so recognized by the party of patriots. Between these claimants for power, a collision soon occurred. The Provincial Congress desired to obtain the removal of the guns on the Battery to the fortifications on the Highlands.

Captain John Lamb, the invincible, was directed by the Provincial Congress to secure their removal, and on the 23d of August proceeded, with some of his faithful liberty boys and other citizens, to execute the order. With his band was Alexander Hamilton, then a lad of eighteen, whose life was dedicated to the sacred cause of freedom.

During the early part of the campaign the Tory party had many friends on Long Island. When the British evacuated Boston through the instrumentality of Washington, who succeeded in compelling them to leave, and occupied their deserted quarters, it was supposed that the defeated Royalists would endeavor to retrieve their fortunes by an effort to gain possession of New York. The policy and actions of the troops were closely watched by Washington, who readily saw that the object was to make New York the seat of government, to surround it with a large force, and thereby cut off all communication with the southern colonies. Thus they expected to divide the country and prevent assistance being sent from one section to another. Had this plan been successfully accomplished a continual fire could have been kept up both north and south. Scouts and rangers would have been used to prey upon the people, doing great damage, and intercourse between the different colonies would have been effectually prevented. In order to avoid this calamity, Washington accepted the offer made by General Lee, who proposed to raise a force for the defense of New York. General Lee immediately collected 1200 efficient men, and proceeded to New York, where he arrived in January, 1776, to the great gratification of the patriots, who did not expect to receive so valuable an addition to their population.

Lee was no novice. A man of executive ability and military skill, he saw at once that energetic measures were necessary in order to tread under foot the existing latent love of royalty, which only needed a little encouragement to burst forth into living activity. It is a singular coincidence that on the very day General Lee entered New York with his forces, the British fleet which had been expected arrived at Sandy Hook, under command of Sir Henry Clinton. The British officer did not seem to like the appearance of things in New York, and for some inexplicable reason changed his course somewhat toward the coast of Virginia.

General Lee had realized the height of his

ambition in being in command of so important a station. At once steps were taken to garrison and fortify the city and its suburbs.

Long Island and Staten Island were justly looked upon as the natural protectors of the harbor of New York, and prudence dictated the advisability of erecting fortifications and posting troops in these localities to watch the approach of belligerent vessels. The patriots were actuated by one spirit, and widely rendered aid and assistance to the heroic commander. Scouts were placed at prominent points at the Narrows, and fortifications erected at Red Hook Point and elsewhere. Some 400 troops were sent to Brooklyn, and performed patrol duty from the settlement at the Wallabout to Gowanus.

Lee was not permitted to remain very long in command in New York, being transferred, March 6, 1776, to the command of the Department of the South. The transfer did not please him. He was possessed of the egotistical idea that the people of New York desired his presence, and believed him to be the only man who could successfully cope with the forces of the enemy. In this he was greatly mistaken. The people were ready to follow any leader who would inspire confidence.

Lee was succeeded by General Lord Stirling, who vigilantly carried on the work initiated by his predecessor. He, too, saw and appreciated the fact that, if New York was to be successfully defended, the approaches on Long Island should be properly garrisoned. To accomplish this desirable end, he appointed Colonel Ward to erect suitable fortifications on Long Island, and placed him in command of a regiment of 519 men.

The second Provincial Congress, which at this time was holding its second session, with Nathaniel Woodhull as president, issued an order to the authorities in Kings County, directing them to give Colonel Ward assistance in the work, and "to turn out for service at least one half the males (negroes included) every day, with spades, hoes, and pickaxes." The inhabitants of Kings County were also required to furnish all the necessary lumber and wood for the barricades and fortifications. The directions given to Colonel Ward were full and explicit. Beside erecting fortifications and providing defenses, he was also required to detail men for the particular duty of preventing communications between the British ships in the harbor and the shore. To make this effectual they either destroyed the small rowboats or rendered them unseaworthy, and seized all suspected pilots who were supposed to be identified with the Royalists by sentiment or self-interest.

Kings County horsemen were honored with the important office of a corps of observation. It became their duty to observe the approach of the British fleet at Sandy Hook from prominent points on Long Island, and to give information of the appearance of suspicious vessels. The Kings County horsemen occupied the west end of the county, and the Brooklyn light horse, under the command of Captain Waldron, were employed on the southern coast of the county, in which service they were employed about a month, when they were relieved by Colonel Hand, April 10, 1776, with a regiment of riflemen. These riflemen took their station at New Utrecht. A battery of eight guns was also erected on Brooklyn Heights.

Onderdonk, referring to Captain Waldron's company, gives the following names of members as being connected with it: Adolph Waldron, captain; William Boerum, first lieutenant; Thomas Everitt, second lieutenant; Jacob Sebring, Jr., cornet; Isaac Sebring, quartermaster; Samuel Etherington, John

Reade, Rob. Galbraithe, Rem. A. Remsen, Daniel Titus, Jos. Smith, Jacob Kempor, Nich. Van Dam, Geo. Powers, William Everitt, John Hicks, William Chardavogne, and Thomas Hazard.

Waldron, the captain of the little company, was a very popular man, and for a long time kept a famous hostelry at the Brooklyn Ferry. During many years he was the proprietor of the ferry between Brooklyn and New York.

William Boerum was a well-known citizen, and has left behind him a host of descendants. After the war he served in the Legislature. George Powers was a butcher, and had a stand at one time in the famous old Fly Market. He owned considerable property in the neighborhood of State and Powers streets. The latter street was named in his honor.

The name of George Powers appears as secretary of the first independent meeting-house erected in Brooklyn in 1785. He was a warm-hearted, generous man, donating large sums to the cause of religion and charity. He retired from business in 1790, and thereafter devoted his time to raising stock on his lands in Brooklyn. It is reported in one of the old journals that in the month of February, 1793, "a calf was brought to the Oswego market (on Broadway and Maiden Lane), yesterday, raised by Mr. George Powers, of Brooklyn, but twenty-two months old, the four quarters of which weighed 744 pounds; hide, 100 pounds; tallow (rough fat), 87 pounds; total, 931 pounds." In March, 1812, the following notice appeared: " Fat Beef for St. Patrick's Day. The three year old steer exhibited at the Coffee House (corner of Wall and Pearl streets), this day, supposed to be one of the best ever seen of his age, and fatted by George Powers, at Brooklyn, will be offered for sale by (one of his apprentices) David Marsh, at No. 38 Fly Market, on Saturday next."

Powers, who was a warm friend of George Hall, the first mayor of Brooklyn, died full of years, honored and respected by all who knew him. The estate he left behind him was estimated to be worth half a million.

John Hicks lived near the ferry, on Fulton Street. He was a large landed proprietor. Hicks Street derives its name from his family. He subsequently was one of the proprietors of the old ferry to New York. The Remsen family were well known in the community. It is a remarkable fact that during the entire time from 1727 to 1776, the Board of Trustees of Kings County had a Rem Remsen for one of its members. A period of fifty years presents a remarkable instance of family succession in one office.

Waldron's troop was first enlisted in the service of General Greene, who ordered them to seize and take possession of all the fat stock of the disaffected inhabitants who sympathized with the Tories, and to deliver the stock so taken to Commissary Brown, on Long Island. The troop was subsequently employed under General Woodhull in the same capacity.

Early in January, 1776, the Continental Congress had passed a resolution, "that it be recommended to the Committee of Safety of the Province of New York to appoint proper persons to inquire into the propriety and practicability of obstructing or lessening the depth of the water in the Narrows, or at any other place at the entrance of New York, or of any way of fortifying that pass so as to prevent the entrance of the enemy."

On the 26th January, 1776, a committee was appointed by the Continental Congress to consult with General Lee and the Committee of Safety in reference to the immediate defense of the province.

The importance of defending and protecting the approaches to the harbor of New York was fully attested by Congress on March 14, 1776, when 8000 men were voted for its defense. On the following day the Governors of Connecticut and New Jersey were requested to hold their militia in readiness for that service, to be paid, when on duty, as Continental troops. Congress went still further, and on the 9th of April directed $200,000 to be sent to New York for the use of the Continental troops in the province.

Previous to its dissolution the second Provincial Congress made provision for the election of delegates to serve in the third Congress of the colony, to meet in the city of New York, May 14, 1776. This election was held in April. At the election so held, Nicholas Cowenhoven, John Lefferts, Lefferts Lefferts, Theodorus Polhemus, Jeremiah Remsen, Rutger Van Brunt, John Vanderbilt, and Jeremiah Vanderbilt were chosen to represent Kings County. Nearly all of these men represented the county in previous assemblies, and were able and experienced legislators.

Prior to the election, and on the 10th of March, a regiment of Continental troops numbering 1000 men took possession of and occupied Governor's Island. They at once constructed a redoubt on the west side of the island, and erected fortifications with a view to holding in check any vessel which might seek an entrance into the harbor. Another regiment was stationed on the shores of Brooklyn, and rendered Red Hook Point, on the north shore of Gowanus Bay, famous as a Revolutionary landmark. At this place a redoubt was also constructed, on which were placed several guns of eighteen-pound calibre. Thus was the entrance to the harbor at two important points effectually protected. This latter fort was appropriately named Fort Defiance. The regiment which was placed here was in command of Captain Foster. The location was not as good as the one on Governor's Island, as vessels were able to make a detour and escape injury from the former, whilst the latter, being so much nearer the city and in the direct sailing course, could more effectually prevent approach.

Shortly afterward (on April 14), Washington, as Commander-in-Chief of the Continental army, arrived in New York and made his headquarters at Richmond Hill, in the neighborhood of Varick Street. His appearance in the city encouraged the patriots to new efforts, quickened their zeal, and led to the completion of the plans so ably instituted by Generals Lee and Stirling. Washington inspired the confidence of the masses, increasing their faith by his earnestness and determination. The strong and confident were rendered more fearless, and the weak and faint-hearted were encouraged to activity.

The people, from a lukewarm and indifferent state, rapidly changed their opinions and became enthusiastic in the cause of independence. These feelings were intensified by numerous newspaper articles and pamphlets which appeared from time to time, denouncing Great Britain and demanding recognition as an independent confederacy. Among these was a paper entitled "Common Sense," by Thomas Paine, then a citizen of Philadelphia. Its author was at the time unknown, but the sentiments of the pamphlet met an approving response in every patriotic heart. Forcible and pointed in expression, its truths left a lasting impression, sending a thrill of pleasure through the community, who heartily approved of its bold and daring utterances. So popular did it become that several of the colonies adopted it as their watchword, and recognizing the force of its reasoning, petitioned the Continental Congress to take immediate steps to secure its ratification by at once declaring themselves free and independent. It was a suitable precursor of the Declaration of Independence, paving the way for the indorsement of that document.

The third Provincial Congress, elected in April, was directed to meet in New York on the 14th of May, but, in consequence of a quorum not being in attendance, the members present adjourned from day to day until the 18th of May, when a quorum having been secured, the body organized and proceeded to business. The session was a short one, continuing only until June 30, when it adjourned by reason of a fear which was entertained that the city would be attacked. Nathaniel Woodhull was elected President of the Congress.

While this body was in session the Continental Congress at Philadelphia was considering important subjects. In the latter body the keynote of independence was struck on the 7th of June, 1776, when General Richard Henry Lee rose in his seat and introduced a resolution declaring " that the united colonies are and ought to be free and independent States, that they are absolved from all allegiance to the British Crown, and that their political connection with Great Britain is and ought to be totally dissolved." The resolution was a surprise to many of the members, and led to an earnest debate which lasted for several weeks. At that time some of the delegates supposed that they were merely banded together for mutual protection, and were not authorized to take so advanced a step without having received instructions from their constituents. In the existing state of affairs many lacked the courage to act, thinking that if they voted in favor of the resolution their action might not meet with the approval of those they represented. They feared also that if the measure were adopted, and in the end proved a failure, they would be called upon to meet a traitor's doom. They were but human. Such men are always to be found in political life. When the prospect of accomplishment looks bright, they are fearless and bold, but when a shadow of disappointment falls, and success is not certain, their courage is weakened, and they are unwilling to lend their aid to what they consider a forlorn hope. The resolution passed by a bare majority. The Congress contained representatives from thirteen colonies, and the vote stood seven in favor to six opposed. This vote, however, did not indicate the exact feeling which existed amongst the members, as those who voted in opposition did so in most if not in all cases because they had received no instructions or directions from their constituents.

The resolution having been passed, a committee, consisting of Thomas Jefferson, John Adams, Benjamin Franklin, Roger Sherman, and Robert R. Livingston, was appointed to prepare and draft a declaration of independence.

Washington was in command in New York about a month, and in the early part of May, 1776, left for Philadelphia. General Putnam was placed in command at New York, and General Greene was assigned to Brooklyn to take charge of the fortifications. Washington was led to visit Philadelphia to consult with the Continental Congress upon the necessary measures to be adopted in order to carry on the campaign. This conference led to the issuance of an order authorizing the commander-in-chief to direct the building of as many fire rafts, galleys, boats, and batteries as might be required for the immediate defense of the port of New York, the Hudson River, and the Sound.

The Provincial Congress of New York, at its session in May, declared the province to be independent of Great Britain, but did not adopt a formal constitution until the following year.

Meanwhile the Continental Congress was not inactive. The committee to which was referred the important duty of drafting the Declaration of Independence worked faithfully, and on the 28th of June, 1776, the paper prepared by Thomas Jefferson was presented for the consideration of the body.

The document was finally adopted on the 4th of July. It was not signed, however, until August. The representatives from New York who signed it were William Floyd of Suffolk County, Philip Livingston of New York, Francis Lewis, who, as we have seen, at one time lived in Brooklyn and owned a large estate there, and Lewis Morris of Westchester. Robert R. Livingston's name should have been appended, but he was called to New York to attend the Provincial Congress before it was engrossed and ready to receive the signatures of the members, and thus his name does not appear on the immortal document. However, as one of its framers he will be forever identified with this glorious manifesto.

Just prior to the adoption of the Declaration, New York was placed in a critical position. On the 23d of June, General Howe with a large fleet appeared before the city, and on the 2d of July took possession of a portion of Staten Island, where he found many adherents of the cause of royalty. Soon after he was joined by his brother, Admiral Lord Howe, with a large fleet from England, and also by Sir Henry Clinton, with the troops under his command. He was thus placed in command of an army consisting of 24,000 well-disciplined men from England. This was not all. The Tory inhabitants flocked to his standard, and although not in many respects as efficient soldiers as the troops from England, still their knowledge of the country rendered them invaluable as aids in prospecting and giving information.

Washington had no such force. To cope with this army he had only 20,000 volunteer recruits, whose knowledge of military tactics was but limited, and many of whom were incapacitated for service. Moreover, had they been disciplined, he had neither the arms nor the ammunition necessary to properly equip them.

Meanwhile provision had been made for the election of delegates to the fourth Provincial Congress of New York. As New York was in a state of siege, it was deemed best to assemble at the court house in White Plains, twenty-six miles from New York. The body met on the 9th of July. Kings County was represented by Theodorus Polhemus. On the first day of the session the Declaration of Independence was read and unanimously adopted. On the following day the title of the body was changed from that of the Provincial Congress of the Colony of New York to that of the Convention of the Representatives of the State of New York. It continued to sit at White Plains until the 27th day of July, when it adjourned to meet at Harlem on the 29th.

It is needless to say that the news of the adoption of the Declaration of Independence occasioned much excitement and enthusiasm in New York and Brooklyn.

Steps were taken to fortify New York and prevent the entry of the enemy. Guns were placed on the Battery, and barricades erected at prominent points on the East and North rivers. The authorities were not content with erecting and planting guns on the water sides, but also appropriated the various hillocks for fortifications. One of these was known as Rutger's, and stood at the brow of the New Bowery, at or near its present junction with Chatham Street. Fortifications and barricades were also constructed at Jersey City and on Brooklyn Heights. The site of Fort Greene, now a beautiful park, was considered a very important position, and a line of works was hastily constructed which extended from the Wallabout to Gowanus Bay, thereby securing a complete chain of defense to the rest of the island.

Within these fortifications 9,000 men were encamped ready to obstruct the approach and forward movements of the English troops. The fortifications on Long Island were erected under the direction of General Greene, who had been assigned to the command of the American forces in this section. General Sullivan, his assistant in the work, rendered valuable aid to his superior officer.

At this time, General Woodhull, who was President of the Representative Convention of New York, feeling that his place was in the saddle, and that he could render better service in the field at the head of troops than in the Legislature, donned his military equipments, and repaired to Long Island to engage in the service.

While the Convention of Representatives was in session at White Plains, a resolution was passed on the 19th of July, requiring that every fourth man in Kings County should be drafted into service. Thereupon the militia of the county sent a letter to the convention urging that body to excuse a draft, and stating that the entire militia would turn out to drive stock into the interior, and also guard the coast line. The letter was signed by the following well-known citizens: John Vanderbilt, Lambert Suydam, Barnet Johnson, John Titus, John Vanderveer, Rem Williamson, Bernardus Suydam, and Adrian Van Brunt, captains.

This request was not granted. The refusal was based upon the fact that, while many of the leading men in the county warmly espoused the patriotic cause, many were disaffected and inclined to the side of royalty. These latter looked upon the war as calculated to unsettle the country and injure their prospects. They thought that under the dominion of the Crown they would have peace, and be enabled to pursue the even tenor of their way undisturbed. The object of the militia in offering their services was to prevent a conscription. It will be noticed that they proposed simply to act as a home guard, and made no pretense of willingness to render general service for the good of the infant nation. Though at the commencement of the war they manifested great lukewarmness, yet this state of feeling was not destined to last very long. The scales were to drop from their eyes, they were to be impressed with a sense of duty, and in the near future make ample amends by courage and fearlessness for the lack of spirit manifested at the commencement.

Among those connected with the Kings County troop of horse, on duty in August, were: Daniel Rapalje, first lieutenant; Jacob Bloom, second lieutenant; Peter Vandervoort, ensign; Honbeck Johnson, sergeant; John Blanco, trumpeter; Roger Suydam and John Vanderveer, privates.

These men went over from Long Island and performed duty in the neighborhood of Harlem. A portion of the troop of horse were stationed on Long Island, being officered as follows: Lambert Suydam, captain; Peter Wyckoff, quartermaster; Hendrick Suydam, clerk; with John Nostrand, Jacob Suydam, Isaac Snedeker, Isaac Boerum, John Ryerson, Rutgert Van Brunt, Charles De Bevoise, Benjamin Seaman, Roelof Terhune, Andrew Casper, Thomas Billing, Martin Kershaw, Peter Miller, and Hendrick Wyckoff, privates.

Amongst these names will be recognized the

ancestors of many of the prominent Wallabout, Bushwick, and Brooklyn families. The Rapaljes, Vandervoorts, Nostrands, Boerums, and Ryersons resided at the Wallabout, and early manifested an interest in the cause of liberty.

The feeling of disaffection on the part of many of the citizens of Long Island was so apparent to the Convention of Representatives that, in refusing the request to exempt them from a draft, that body considered it necessary to appoint a committee to visit Kings County for the purpose of ascertaining the true state of public feeling in the county, with power to take from all disaffected citizens such arms as they might possess, to secure their persons, and, if deemed necessary, "to destroy the crops and lay the whole country waste," and thus prevent them from affording aid and comfort to the enemy. The committee entered upon their labors with energy and dispatch. They ascertained that the reports were in a great measure true. By their direction Tories were arrested and disarmed. The action of the committee produced a beneficial effect amongst the people, and, had they not taken the forcible measures they did, the first battle of the Revolution after the Declaration of Independence, which was fought on Long Island soon after, to wit, on the 27th day of August, would in its results have proved still more disastrous.

General Greene made ample provision to protect and defend Long Island against the enemy. As we have already seen, he caused a line of fortifications to be constructed through the centre of the present city of Brooklyn, extending from Wallabout Bay on the north to Gowanus Bay on the south.

Conspicuous among the fortifications so constructed was the redoubt on Fort Greene, which was called Fort Putnam in honor of that brave officer General Israel Putnam, who figured with distinction not only in Brooklyn but elsewhere, and subsequently gained for himself the name of Breakneck Putnam for his daring exploit in Connecticut when he dashed down the celebrated defile, and thereby escaped capture.

At this time Fort Putnam, now Washington Park (Fort Greene), was covered with large trees, and belonged to the Cowenhoven estate. The old Bedford Road skirted its northeasterly line, and its prominence was a valuable position for placing guns. It is worthy of note in this connection that Edward T. Backhouse, a descendant by marriage of the original owner, when representing the old eleventh ward of Brooklyn in the Common Council, in the middle of the present century, took an active interest in securing the preservation of this historic spot and its conversion into a place of public resort. He aided materially, with Francis B. Stryker, late Mayor, Silas Ludlow, John W. Hunter, John H. Baker, and others, in having it set apart for a park, and properly embellished.

Another means of protection was the construction of intrenchments extending from Fort Putnam to the old Wallabout Road, at a point about where Hampden Street intersects the present line of Flushing Avenue. Before Flushing Avenue was opened, at this point, the easterly end of the Navy Yard property, the old Wallabout Road diverged from its course, describing a half circle.

General Greene was not content with providing against invasion from the northeast, but also turned his attention to the section lying to the south of Fort Greene. He saw the necessity of erecting intrenchments along the high land extending from Fulton Avenue southerly to the old Gowanus Road, at the creek which made up from the bay where

Freeck's mill stood. This spot can be easily fixed. Many remember the old mill pond and the bridge across the creek at Butler Street, near where Bond Street has been extended.

Another small redoubt, which stood like a warning sentinel, was erected a short distance west of the fort, about where DeKalb Avenue now intersects Hudson Avenue. South Brooklyn was not forgotten. At that time the section bounded by Smith and Clinton streets on the east, and Degraw and Third Place on the north, was high ground, and from its owner's name was called Bergen Hill. This prominence commanded a view of the East River and Gowanus Bay. Here Greene erected a redoubt, on which he mounted several guns. In later times, when the hill was removed, to give place to streets and palatial residences, the remains of soldiers buried during the Revolutionary War were taken up. A fort was also built on Cobble Hill, which was nick-named "Corkscrew Fort." This hill was on the spot where since has been erected the Athenæum, corner of Clinton and Atlantic streets.

All these works were effectively built and evinced great military and engineering skill. English officers at the time of the evacuation referred to their strength of material and advantageous location. It would appear that Greene and his assistants thoroughly familiarized themselves with the topography of the country, and made military provision accordingly. A British officer, in his experiences published during the war, expressed in strong terms his surprise that the Americans should retreat from bastions so impregnable.

Hitherto all had been preparation. The storm clouds had been gathering, and were soon to break with unwonted fury. A great Revolutionary battle was to be fought on the virgin soil of Long Island, and was to result disastrously.

At the outset, Great Britain, having complications on the European continent, was very anxious to conciliate and secure peace. When Admiral Howe was sent with his fleet to New York he was directed by his government to treat for peace with the rebellious subjects. Acting upon his instructions, after landing at Staten Island, and placing his fleet in close proximity to the city, he opened negotiations to this end. At the start he made a great blunder, by mistaking the character of the general-in-chief with whom he had to deal. An autocrat in temper and disposition, and infused with the traditional pride of a British commander, he neglected to address Washington by his military title. He looked upon the people as rebels, and not as an independent nation, and addressed the commander of the American forces as George Washington, Esq. The letter was returned unanswered. Another missive directed to George Washington, Esq., met the same fate. The spirit thus manifested by Washington in refusing to receive or reply to any letters, unless addressed to him as the head of an independent army, representing a nation seeking to throw off the yoke of despotism and break its chains, proved to Admiral Howe that his mission of peace was too late, and that if England desired to retain her possessions in the new world she would have to do so at the point of the bayonet.

Howe made his last effort to secure peace on the 17th day of August. Failing, he at once commenced warlike preparations. Washington realized the necessity of careful and energetic action. He anticipated that the rebuff he had administered to the admiral's overtures would lead to an immediate attack upon New York. In order to circumvent the attack, and prevent aid and assistance to the enemy from the Tories in the city, he at once caused the removal of the adherents of the Crown to Connecticut, where they were placed under the surveillance of that sturdy patriot, Governor Trumbull. Measures were adopted to weaken and destroy existing Tory sentiments in New Jersey and Long Island. The legislative committee, assisted by a committee from the Continental Congress, went to work to disarm all suspected persons on Long Island, and to suppress every exhibition of Tory spirit. The public records were placed in the care of Congress, then in session in Philadelphia; and women and children, and all persons not needed for the defense of the city, were quickly removed to safe quarters. A corps of riflemen was stationed at Fort Hamilton to prevent the landing of the enemy in that quarter, to watch the approach of their fleet, and to give information as to their movements.

Washington, however, was mistaken as to the intentions of the enemy. Howe, instead of making a bold attack upon New York, resolved upon another course. He well knew that Long Island was filled with Tory sympathizers, and he thought that he might reach New York across Long Island, and be able to take with him many recruits gathered on his way from among the disloyal inhabitants. Within five days after the refusal of Washington to reply to his insulting letter, Howe prepared his fleet for action, and with it set sail for Gravesend Bay, where he landed on August 22.

The fleet arrived early in the morning. General Sir William Howe led an army of 30,000 well-disciplined soldiers. The landing was effected without opposition. A part of the forces was under the command of Earls Cornwallis and Percy, Sir William Erskine, Count Duness, and Generals Grant, De Heister, and Knyphausen, and was composed of many Hessians who had been hired at a set price per head to do military service against the American rebels.

Howe held possession of the southwestern part of the Island. His presence caused consternation among the patriots, who sought the American lines for protection, while those who were weak in the faith, or favored the cause of royalty, joined his standard.

The small body of riflemen who had been stationed at Fort Hamilton could not prevent the landing of the invaders. They, however, destroyed the growing crops so that the enemy would derive no benefit from the cereals, and, having done this, sought safe quarters between Brooklyn and Flatbush. Meanwhile Howe was not idle. Establishing his headquarters at New Utrecht, he employed his men in reconnoitring. Skirmishers were sent out from time to time, who succeeded in capturing many straggling soldiers, and withal securing much plunder. General Sullivan, who was in command of the American forces, had but 5000 men. These lacked the ability to contend against the numbers opposed to them. Most of Sullivan's men were volunteers, unused to the hardships of camp life, and without experience in military tactics. Notwithstanding the disparity of numbers, Sullivan made diligent preparation to resist the onward progress of the enemy should they attempt to press forward to New York. Washington at this time was with the main body in New York, laboring earnestly to defend the lines of that city, and obstruct the progress of the enemy should they attempt to lay siege to the town.

On the 25th of August Washington sent large reinforcements to Brooklyn. At the same time General Sullivan was removed from the command of the army, and General Putnam dispatched to take his place. Washington supposed that the enemy would attack Long Island and New York at the same time. Putnam on assuming command received strict injunctions to guard all the passes, and thereby prevent advance movements on the part of Howe. Sullivan had planned the intrenchments, and having studied the ground in conjunction with General Greene, he knew where to station his sentinels. The country was thickly covered with wood from the Narrows to Jamaica. The American camp could be reached only by three accessible passes. One of these wound round the western edge of the Narrows; another crossed the range to Flatbush; and the other passed through Flatlands, crossing the Bedford and Jamaica roads. Sullivan had erected breastworks near these passes, and at each stationed several regiments. Scouts were also employed to watch the roads leading to the passes, and give the alarm in case the enemy approached. Putnam did not manifest much ability upon taking command of the army. Instead of strengthening the outposts, which were a sure protection against the progress of the enemy and the annihilation of his camp, and which had been wisely chosen by his predecessor, he saw fit to remove the patrol, and thereby weakened his own position, gave the enemy an unobstructed road to the American camp, and insured the disaster which attended the battle that followed, causing demoralization not only in his own ranks, but also throughout the entire army, which in a great measure became disheartened by the terrible defeat on Long Island. Had General Greene, who had served as the superior officer to Sullivan, not been prostrated by sickness, and been enabled to remain in command, instead of being replaced by Putnam, no such disaster would have occurred. He knew the character of the country, and the importance of holding the passes, and would not have readily yielded up their possession.

Meanwhile General Howe, the commander of the British forces, issued a proclamation, wherein he gave notice, on behalf of his Majesty's government, to all persons who had been forced into rebellion, that, on delivering themselves up at the headquarters of the army, they would be received as faithful subjects, and be given permission to return to their dwellings, and be protected in person and property. And further, that "all those who choose to take up arms for the restoration of order and good government within this Island shall be disposed of in the best manner, and have every encouragement that can be expected." This offer was accepted by some lukewarm people; but to the honor of the majority be it said, its terms and conditions were, in general, indignantly refused.

General Clinton, whose forces had joined those of Howe, soon saw the unprotected state of the passes. The information he acquired as to their unguarded condition he at once communicated to Howe, who thereupon held a consultation with him, and planned measures to entrap the patriots. They arranged a plan of attack. On the 26th the Hessian troops, under command of General De Heister, took the road leading to Flatbush through the hills, while General Grant, with another division, took the shore road. These movements were intended to deceive Putnam, and enable General Clinton, with the main body, to direct his efforts to gain possession of the pass at Bedford, and thereby flank the American lines. The manœuvre was successful. Putnam, learning of the advance of Generals De Heister and Grant, dispatched a strong force under Lord Stirling to guard the river road, and another under General Sullivan to impede the progress of De Heister at Flatbush. Putnam did not comprehend the movements of the enemy, and did not learn the advantage they had gained by their military skill until General Clinton had accomplished his purpose, by gaining the position he desired, and had opened a heavy fire upon Sullivan's rear. Sullivan saw that he was surrounded. After vainly attempting to break through the lines of the enemy and secure the lost ground, his troops became confused and broke ranks, taking refuge in the neighboring hills. They could not escape, and the greater part, with their faithful officer, were soon discovered and secured as prisoners of war.

The contest with General Grant on the shore road was far more animated and vigorous. Lord Stirling, who had command of the American troops, was posted on the slope of the hills just north of Greenwood Cemetery, and firmly maintained his ground against Grant, until the latter received reinforcements. Early on the morning of the 27th, General Grant reached the lower pass, and encountering a regiment under command of Major Bird, was compelled to retreat. General Putnam, who had been apprised of the retreat, directed Lord Stirling to hold the invaders in check. Stirling, in obedience to the order, started with two regiments for the Narrows. A Connecticut regiment was also placed under marching orders, and followed to render him support and assistance.

Stirling soon met Major Bird retreating before the fire of the enemy. He formed his brigade in line of battle, judiciously placing some of his men on the brow of the hills in order to rake the enemy with hot shot. Another body was stationed near "Battle Hill," now a portion of Greenwood. It is said that some riflemen were stationed on this eminence, and, when Earl Cornwallis approached with his command, these riflemen commenced a deadly fire, each shot proving the death-blow of an officer. Their aim was so effective and disastrous that they could not long escape. The bravery manifested by these men cost each one his life, as the hill was quickly surrounded, and the sure marksmen dispatched. Furman has graphically pictured this event. He says: "In this battle part of the British army marched down a lane or road, leading from the British tavern (at Valley Forge) to Gowanus, pursuing the Americans. Several of the American riflemen, in order to be more secure, and at the same time more effectually to succeed in their designs, had posted themselves in the high trees near the road; one of them, whose name is now partially forgotten, shot the English Major Grant; in this he passed unobserved. Again he leveled his deadly rifle and fired; another English officer fell. He was then marked, and a platoon ordered to advance and fire into the tree, which order was immediately carried into execution, and the rifleman fell to the ground dead. After the battle was over, the two British officers were buried in a field near where they fell, and their graves fenced in with some posts and rails, where their remains still rest. But 'for an example to the rebels,' they refused to the American rifleman the rites of sepulchre; and his remains were exposed on the ground till the flesh was rotted and torn off his bones by the fowls of the air. After a considerable length of time, in a heavy gale of wind, a large tree was uprooted; in the cavity formed by which some friends to the Americans, notwithstanding the prohibition of the English, placed the brave soldier's bones to mingle in peace with their kindred earth."

Before the beginning of this attack, General Stirling addressed his men, urging them to be courageous, and told them: " Grant may have his 5000 men with him now;— we are not so many; but I think we are enough to prevent his advance further on his march than that mill-pond."

The battle soon started in earnest. As the golden sun on that August day slowly uplifted itself above the horizon, and began its movement towards the west, the armies were engaged in deadly conflict. Skirmishing continued for two hours. The fire from Kichline's riflemen, who were stationed behind a hedge, proved disastrous to the British, who were compelled in consequence to relinquish their position. No sooner did they retire than a Pennsylvania regiment under Atlee retook the lost ground.

Stirling was now closely pressed by General Grant, whose brigade had formed in two lines opposite Stirling's right. Stirling soon saw that Grant had been reinforced, and felt that further resistance would be in vain. He had but two courses to adopt: one was to surrender at once, or attempt to escape across the creek, which was spanned by the remains of a burnt mill-dam. Preferring to make an effort to escape, he selected a portion of the Maryland brigade to cover his flight, and directed the balance to retreat. With great courage he then charged with fixed bayonets upon the regiments commanded by Cornwallis. The charge was repeated four times. Again they charged, and as the enemy was on the point of yielding, General De Heister came up, flushed with his victory over Sullivan, and commenced an assault on his rear. With such a force against him Stirling was compelled to surrender. Some attempted to escape by cutting their way through the ranks of the enemy, and perished in the effort. The Americans lost in this battle 1200 men, 1000 of whom, including Lord Stirling and General Sullivan, were taken prisoners. About 400 of the British were killed, wounded, and taken prisoners.

Historians have always differed as to the loss of the Americans in the battle of Brooklyn. Colonel Trumbull was commissary-general during the engagement, and was employed, when the retreat was determined upon, in procuring vessels in which to remove the army. By virtue of his position he possessed peculiar facilities for knowing the true state of affairs. Two days after the retreat he wrote the following letter to his father, giving an account of Washington's masterly effort:

NEW YORK, September 1, 1776.

HONORED SIR, — We have been obliged to retreat from Long Island and Governor's Island, from both of which we got off without loss of men. We left a great part of our heavy artillery behind. The field train is off. We are in hourly expectation that the town will be bombarded and cannonaded, and the enemy are drawing their men to the eastward of Long Island, as if they intended to throw a strong party over on this island, near Hell Gate, so as to get on the back of the city. We are preparing to meet them. Matters appear to be drawing near a decisive engagement. General Sullivan is allowed to come on shore, upon his parole, and go to Congress, on the subject of exchange of himself, Lord Stirling, and a large number who are prisoners; by the best accounts we yet have, we have lost in last week's defeat about 800 men killed and missing; how many of each is not yet known. I rather expect that they will push in a body of troops between the town and our party at and near Kingsbridge. If they do, we shall have them between two fires, and must push them to the last extremity, or be killed or taken prisoners. The result is in the hands of the Almighty Disposer of all events.

I am, honored sir, your dutiful son,

JOSEPH TRUMBULL.

While the battle was raging with so much fury, Washington was in New York, watching the movements of the British fleet. He was filled with anxiety and alarm, as he considered that an important crisis had arrived. Becoming satisfied during the day that there was no intention on the part of the fleet to attack the city, he passed over to Brooklyn and took his station at Fort Putnam.

Here he witnessed the terrible rout and slaughter which befell Sullivan, with no means at his command to send succor or assistance. He also beheld the heroic conduct of the men under Stirling, and was convinced that resistance on their part was in vain. As Washington noticed the bravery of the Maryland troops in the bayonet charge, he exclaimed, "Good God, what brave fellows I must this day lose."

Thus terminated the battle on the 27th. The slaughter had been terrible on both sides. The flower of the American army was destroyed, and many valuable and efficient officers were taken prisoners. General Howe felt jubilant over his success, and made preparations to advance upon the American lines. Within those lines were 3000 brave men who were encouraged by the presence of Washington. Had an attempt been made to take their fortifications, they would not have been yielded without the destruction of hosts of the invaders. As Howe did not know the strength of the

Americans, he deemed it prudent not to make the attempt, and encamped for the night. It was not singular, under the circumstances, that Washington should feel alarmed. He was satisfied that resistance would be useless, and that something must be done to save the remnant of his army.

The Hessians, who had been hired by the British Government, were trained soldiers. Of the men so procured the Landgrave of Hesse Cassel furnished 12,000 infantry, the Duke of Brunswick 3900, and the Count of Hanau 360. War was their profession, and in its destructive work they seemed to take great delight. In the engagements on Long Island they took an active part, and manifested their disposition by showing no quarter. The sight of blood served to madden them, and led them on to renewed acts of diabolism and ferocity. Nothing satisfied their rapacity. After the retreat of the Americans from Long Island, and its occupation by the British, many of these Hessians took possession of and were quartered in the large old-fashioned Dutch houses, and made themselves free with everything on which they could lay their hands.

The morning of the 28th of August arrived. A thick mist enshrouded the earth with gloom.

Washington did not manifest any despondency, and as he inspected the works and defenses had a cheerful word of encouragement for the men. Early in the morning several regiments of Massachusetts soldiers crossed to the island, and were received with manifestations of joy by the weary toilers of the day and night past. With this addition the force of the Americans numbered 9000 men. The battle was now renewed by the British, who commenced a heavy cannonade on the American works. Providence seemed to smile upon the American cause. The clouds poured forth rain in torrents, which, while it produced much physical discomfort to the patriots, who were compelled to stand knee deep in water, served also to restrain and prevent the enemy from engaging in the conflict.

Washington realized the necessity of immediate action. A council of officers was summoned, and by his advice the conclusion was reached to evacuate the island. The council convened by Washington to deliberate upon this important subject was composed of the commander-in-chief, General Washington; major generals Putnam and Spencer, brigadier generals Mifflin, McDougall, Parsons, Scott, Wadsworth, and Fellows. In Stiles's account of the battle of Long Island, he says that "the old Cornell House, afterwards known as the Pierrepont Mansion, which formerly stood on the line of the present Montague Street, near the little iron footbridge which spans the carriageway, was the headquarters of Washington during this important contest. It was a spacious and costly house having large chimneys, from which it was known as the 'Four Chimneys;' and upon its roof a telegraph was arranged by which communication was held with New York."

Stiles maintains that both Lossing and Onderdonk erred in stating that the council met in the Dutch church on Fulton Street, but that they met in this old house. In supporting his opinion he quotes the authority of Colonel Fish, the father of Governor Hamilton Fish, and one of Washington's military family, who in 1824, during Lafayette's visit to Brooklyn, called the attention of the distinguished visitor to the fact, and designated the very positions in the room occupied by the members of that council.

The business brought before the council was very important, and the execution of the scheme adopted required military skill and strategy to insure success. It would not have answered to retreat during the day, as their movements would have been noticed and checkmated by the enemy. It was resolved to effect the withdrawal of the troops that night. Every move required the utmost caution and secrecy. As boats were needed to transport the troops, and the collecting together of them might excite the suspicion of the British, it was reported that the Americans intended to attack the enemy in the rear, and to accomplish this end had determined to transport troops to the line of Queens County at Hell Gate. This plan was adopted to deceive the enemy. In pursuance of the resolution of the council, orders were issued to move every available boat to Brooklyn, and have them in readiness for embarkation at midnight. So cautious were the officers conducting this retreat that all orders were given in whispers, and communicated to the men in the same manner. The state of the weather favored the movements of Washington. During the day rain had fallen in copious showers. As the mantle of night covered the earth, a heavy fog appeared, which, with the drizzling mist, served to deceive the enemy, and render them less vigilant. In order to mislead the British officers and soldiers, Washington kept several companies marching to and from the ferry landing, while their associates were embarking. Washington himself superintended the embarkation of the troops, who began to move about ten o'clock. The darkness of the night aided materially in the accomplishment of the work. To add to the deception, fires were kept burning until the last moment. All the troops were safely embarked. The boatmen labored cheerfully during the night watches, and when at last the fog passed away, and they beheld the clear cerulean sky above them, they also rejoiced that a kind Providence had directed their boats to a safe harbor on the shores of the upper part of the city of New York.

The elements, time, and circumstances, favored Washington in his masterly retreat. On one side he had to fear the forces of Howe, who might pursue and cut off his retreat, and on the other hand, if he succeeded in putting off from the land, he stood in imminent danger from the British fleet, which, if his movements were discovered, would soon send him and his faithful band to a watery grave. Again, he was liable to be exposed by some stray British soldier or spy.

A woman Tory, Mrs. Rapalje, living near

the ferry, noticing the collection of boats and the movements of the troops, suspected that a retreat had been determined. Anxious to apprise her friends, the Tories, of the undertaking, she at once sent her negro slave to give General Clinton the information. Fortunately for Washington, the slave was captured by a Hessian soldier, who, not understanding the English language, could not comprehend the importance of the message, and kept the slave in the guard-house until morning, when he sent him to Clinton's headquarters. When Clinton received the message the birds had flown.

The story was communicated to Howe, who received it with blank astonishment. At first he could not accept it as true. The scouts reported that a dead silence rested upon the American camp. Howe now feared that the story might be too true, and that, " while he slumbered and slept," Washington had escaped. At last one of the guard crept close to the works, and found that they had been abandoned. The alarm was given, the crestfallen British took possession, and, like Pharaoh of old, pursued, to find that those they sought had landed safely on the other side.[1]

[1] The wife of John Rapalje was a well-known Tory. So far did she manifest her predilections in favor of the Tory

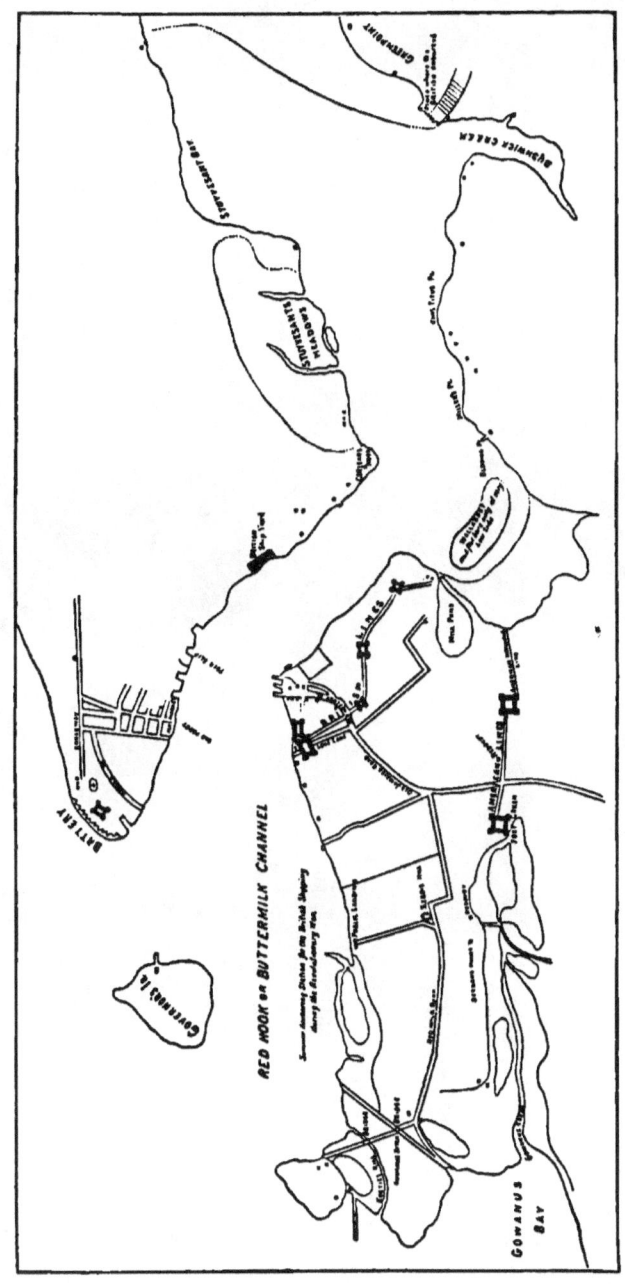

BROOKLYN DURING THE REVOLUTIONARY WAR

From the map by Gen. Jeremiah Johnson

Howe now took possession of the deserted works. All the towns of Kings County were in possession of the army, who had strong garrisons in each. Meantime Howe made his headquarters at Newtown. During the continuance of the war thereafter, and for a period of over seven years, Kings County remained under the absolute control and domination of the British.

Howe now made another effort to restore the colonies to the mother country. The disaster and repulse which the Americans received in Brooklyn led him to suppose it a favorable opportunity to accomplish his mission of peace. He communicated with the Continental Congress, and opened negotiations with a promise of pardon to all who

cause as at all times to boldly proclaim her sympathies for the King. At the time the act was passed prohibiting the use of tea, she, with her proverbial pertinacity and obstinacy, persisted in its use, and so continued while the American army was in the occupation of Brooklyn. On this account she became a marked woman. Her conduct caused much discussion, and drew down upon her the umbrage of the Whig militia, who fired a cannon ball into her home while she was drinking her favorite beverage. The ball passed close to her head and lodged in the wall. This action not only seriously annoyed the lady, but served to stir within her bosom the spirit of revenge, and she eagerly awaited an opportunity to gratify her spite. When she saw the preparations for the retreat of the army her heart rejoiced, for she fancied that the moment had arrived when she could mete out punishment to her enemies.
— S. M. O.

would lay down their arms. He also added a promise that the obnoxious laws which had led to the struggle should be repealed.

The proposition came too late. No concession but acknowledgment of independence would satisfy the people. A conference was held at Staten Island, whereat Benjamin Franklin, John Adams, and Francis Rutledge, the commissioners appointed by Congress to attend the negotiations, refused to listen to any terms of peace, except such as should recognize the full and complete independence of the colonies. Howe, having failed in his effort, issued another proclamation to the people, and resolved to proceed and take the city of New York.

The battle of Brooklyn cost the Americans the loss of that brave general, Nathaniel Woodhull, who for nearly a year had acted as the President of the Provincial Congress of New York. He was in command of a part of the forces, and was captured on the 28th of August by a party of Tories under command of Captain De Lancey, near the village of Jamaica. Notwithstanding the fact that he was a prisoner, and entitled to respectful treatment, he suffered great indignities at the hands of his captors, who inflicted numerous sabre wounds, which resulted in his death. He was at first taken to the Presbyterian Church in Jamaica, where for the night he was confined with other patriots. In the morning he was placed on a hay-boat, and taken down Jamaica Bay to New York Bay, and landed at New Utrecht. Reaching the latter place he began to fail very rapidly, and the officers, seeing his days were numbered, allowed him to be carried to the house of Nicasius De Sille, where he died as a true soldier, breathing blessings on his countrymen, and willingly giving his life in the cause he loved so well.

Woodhull was the hero of Long Island. He rendered important service in the formation of the state government, and was always a leader who secured and retained the respect and confidence of his constituents.

The occupation of Long Island by the British did not accomplish the results anticipated. The victory gained was barren. The authorities at home did not see in it anything to commend. In the light of present knowledge it was passing strange that Generals Howe and Clinton and Admiral Howe should have committed so fatal a blunder as to attempt the subjugation of the city of New York by a passage of the army across Long Island. The situation of Manhattan Island, extending into the bay, with a wide expanse of water on each side, presented an inviting field for an attack upon the city. Admiral Howe, with his large and well-equipped fleet, could have readily besieged New York, and forced Washington with his little band of patriots to evacuate the place. As it was he weakened his force, and enabled Washington to concentrate his army. Long Island being isolated from the main land was of but little consequence to either side. Had Howe with his fleet besieged the city, and landed the military forces, their success would have been complete, as the Americans were not prepared to resist the invasion. Such a policy would have resulted disastrously to the patriotic cause. As we have already stated, the battle of Brooklyn was never looked upon by British authorities as at all creditable. Whatever glory gathers round the engagement centres in the exhibition of military skill displayed by Washington in the management of the masterly retreat of the American army from Long Island, and its safe arrival in the city of New York.

Yet Washington was greatly distressed and disheartened by the defeat at Brooklyn. In referring to the battle in one of his letters written shortly after the disaster, he expressed his feelings in unmistakable terms. He says: " The check our detachment sustained on the 27th has disappointed too great a proportion of our troops and filled their minds with apprehension and despair. The militia, instead of calling forth their utmost efforts to a brave and manly opposition, in order to repair our losses, are dismayed, intractable, and impatient to return. Great numbers of them have gone off! in some instances by whole regiments, by half ones, and by companies, at a time." Washington was well-nigh discouraged by the state of affairs. He had enlisted with the purest motives, and ever manifested a spirit of self-sacrifice. He regretted that the same spirit did not abide with those who had with him enlisted in the service.

Howe, having full possession of the American fortifications on Long Island, determined to use the fleet under command of his brother, Admiral Howe. The vessels were brought within gunshot of the city. The Rose, carrying forty guns, passed through Buttermilk Channel and anchored in Turtle Bay, in the neighborhood of Forty-second Street and East River, to aid the other vessels then in the Sound by a concert of action against the city.

Washington, noticing the movements of the ships of war, and foreseeing that the condition of his army would not permit a defense, resolved to leave the city. Before doing so he summoned a council of his officers, who coincided with him in his views of the situation. This was on the 12th of September. An order was issued at once for the removal of the military stores across the Harlem River, and a force was stationed at Kingsbridge.

General Putnam was left in command of the city with about 4000 men. The main body under Washington was stationed at Harlem Heights. Washington was now surrounded with difficulties which required great ability to overcome. The enemy had the men and means to move on his works, and against their attack he could offer but feeble resistance. It was a dark and doleful hour in our history. In order to make no mistake it became necessary to adopt a decisive policy, and to arrange plans whereby the advance movements of the enemy might be circumvented. He considered it of the utmost importance to ascertain the intentions of Howe and Clinton. A council of war was called, and it was resolved to send a man who could be trusted into the enemy's ranks to gain the desired information.

In this emergency Nathan Hale, a young and brilliant officer, volunteered his services. Procuring the necessary disguise, Hale started on the mission fraught with so much danger. Passing over to Long Island, he entered unnoticed and unobserved the enemy's line, succeeded in making drawings of their works, and gained full and complete information as to all their intended movements.

As he was returning, he was recognized as belonging to the rebel army, and was arrested, and conveyed to the Beekman house, on the corner of Fifty-first Street and First Avenue, where General Howe had his headquarters. He was at once tried, convicted as a spy, and sentenced to be hung on the following day at daybreak. It was a mercy to him that his execution was fixed so speedily, as in the mean time he was placed in the keeping of that heartless scoundrel, Cunningham, whose after deeds as provost marshal of New York have rendered his name forever infamous. Hale was kept in confinement during the night by the marshal, who refused to give him a light and writing materials to enable him to send a last message of love to his aged parents and friends. A kindly disposed lieutenant afterwards furnished him with pen and paper. Cunningham, however, in the morning manifested the natural atrocity of his disposition by rudely tearing into pieces before his eyes the letters which he had written, and at the same time declaring "that the rebels should never know that they had a man in their army who could die with so much firmness."

On the morning of September 22, 1776, Cunningham ordered the execution to proceed, and at the same time required Hale to make a dying confession. In the nobility of his liberty-loving nature, Hale said: "I only regret that I have but one life to lose for my country." These brave words were his last. He was suspended on an apple-tree, and his remains were committed to the grave without any ceremony. He did not perish; his name will live as that of one of the heroes of the Revolution. In the American army he was universally beloved, and his untimely end filled the hearts of his friends with deep-seated hatred to their foes, and a renewed determination to be avenged.

In this connection the following may not be uninteresting. It is an extract from a letter from New York, dated September 1, 1776:[1]

"Last Monday we went over to Long Island,

---

[1] Force's 5th series, vol. ii. p. 107.

and about midnight we were alarmed by the return of some of our scouting parties, who advised us that the *English* were in motion, and coming up the island with several field pieces; it was generally thought not to be the main body, but only a detachment, with a view to possess themselves of some advantageous heights, upon which near three thousand men were ordered out, consisting chiefly of the Pennsylvania and Maryland troops, to attack them on their march. The Delaware and Maryland battalions made one party. Colonel Atlee with his battalion, a little before us, had taken post in an orchard, and behind a barn, and on the approach of the enemy he gave them a very severe fire, which he bravely kept up for a considerable time, until they were near surrounding him, when he retreated to the woods. The enemy then advanced towards us, upon which *Lord Stirling*, who commanded, immediately drew us up in line, and offered them battle in the true *English* taste. The British army then advanced within three hundred yards of us, and began a heavy fire from their cannon and mortars, for both the balls and shells flew very fast, now and then taking off a head. Our men stood it amazing well; not even one of them showed a disposition to shrink.

"Our orders were not to fire until the enemy came within fifty yards of us; but when they perceived we stood their fire so coolly and resolutely, they declined coming any nearer, though treble our number. In this situation we stood from sunrise to twelve o'clock, the enemy firing upon us the chief part of the time, when the main body of their army, by a route we never dreamed of, had utterly surrounded us, and drove within the lines or scattered in the woods all our men except the *Delaware* and Maryland battalions, who were standing at bay with double their number. Thus situated, we were ordered to attempt a retreat by fighting our way through the enemy, who had posted themselves and nearly filled every field and road between us and our lines. We had not retreated a quarter of a mile before we were fired upon by an advanced party of the enemy, and those upon our rear were playing upon us with their artillery. Our men fought with more than *Roman* courage, and I am convinced would have stood until they were shot down to a man. We forced the advanced party which first attacked us to give way, through which opening we got a passage down to the side of a marsh, seldom before waded over, which we passed, and then swam a narrow river, all the time exposed to the fire of the enemy. The companies commanded by Captains Ramsey and Scott were in the front, and sustained the first fire of the enemy, when hardly a man fell.

"The whole right wing of our battalion, thinking it impossible to pass through the marsh, attempted to force their way through the woods, where they were almost to a man killed or taken. The Maryland battalion has lost two hundred and fifty-nine men, amongst whom are twelve officers: Captains Veazey and Bowie, the first certainly killed; Lieutenants Butler, Sterritt, Dent, Coursey, Muse, Prawl; Ensigns Coates and Fernandez; who of them killed or who prisoners is yet uncertain. Many of the officers lost their swords and guns. We have since abandoned Long Island, bringing off all our military stores.

"Generals Sullivan and Stirling are both prisoners. Colonels Atlee, Miles, and Piper are also taken. There are about one thousand men missing in all. We took a few prisoners. By a lieutenant we took, we understand they had about twenty-three thousand men on the Island that morning. Most of our Generals were upon a high hill, in our lines, viewing us with glasses. When we began our retreat, they could see the enemy we had to pass through, though we could not. Many of them thought we would surrender in a body without firing. When we begun the attack, General *Washington* wrung his hands and cried out, *Good God! What brave fellows I must this day lose.* Major Guest commanded the *Maryland* battalion, the Colonel and Lieutenant Colonel being both at York. Captains Adams and Lucas were sick. The Major, Captain Ramsey and Lieutenant Plunkett were foremost and within forty yards of the enemy's muzzles, when they were fired upon by the enemy, who were chiefly under cover of an orchard, save a force that showed themselves, and pretended to give up, clubbing their firelocks until we came within that distance, when they immediately presented, and blazed in our faces; they entirely overshot us, and killed some men away behind in our rear. I had the satisfaction of dropping one of them the first fire I made. I was so near I could not miss. I discharged my rifle seven times that day, as deliberately as I ever did at a mark, and with as little perturbation."

Washington, in a letter dated September 4, 1776, addressed to General Schuyler, fixes the number in killed, wounded, and prisoners on the American side in the Long Island battle at from seven hundred to one thousand men.[1]

In writing to the Massachusetts Assembly, under date of September 19, 1776, Washington states that the number in killed and wounded of the enemy could not be ascertained, "but that it was pretty considerable and exceeded ours a good deal." He also says that the Americans lost eight hundred men, three fourths of whom were taken prisoners, thereby leaving only two hundred killed.[2]

English writers upon this subject place the loss on the American side at between three and four thousand. These figures greatly overstep the mark, and were doubtless gathered from the reports of those commanding generals who desired to make it appear to the home authorities that a substantial victory had been secured.

The loss in the battle of Brooklyn is fixed by the best authorities at not over a thousand men. This, as we have seen, is the number fixed by Washington himself, both in his letters and official reports. Johnson, in his admirable and exhaustive narrative of the campaign of 1776, concurs in this view. These figures appear to

---
[1] Force, 5th series, vol. ii. p. 167.
[2] Force, 5th series, vol. ii. p. 399.

be a correct estimate of the loss sustained. Certainly if as many had been killed as reported by British officials, some tradition or evidence would exist as to the vast number requiring burial after the battle, and subsequent to the evacuation. The neutral inhabitants remaining on the island would have found abundant occupation in consigning so many to mother earth. This alone would have rendered the occasion memorable.

The loss on the Tory side appears from the returns made by General Howe to have been:— Commissioned officers: three generals, three colonels, four lieutenant-colonels, three majors, eighteen captains, forty-three lieutenants, and eleven ensigns; staff officers: one adjutant, three surgeons, two volunteers; privates: one thousand and six. This includes nine wounded officers and fifty-six wounded privates.[1]

In the annals of the Revolutionary period in Brooklyn, a conspicuous place is occupied by the famous Rising Sun tavern. It stood (and still stands) at the junction of the Bedford and Jamaica turnpikes in East New York, and was an old-fashioned farm-house of the Dutch type. This famous tavern, from its prominent position on the King's highway,

---

[1] Force, 5th series, vol. iii. p. 1057.

was a resort for the burghers and farmers of the island. The host, William Howard, was very popular amongst the people, and the old landmark, so prominent in the early history of Kings County, has long been an object of interest.

At this house, the day before the battle of Brooklyn, an important meeting in reference to the war was held. The house was situated within five miles of the American intrenchments, which were in the neighborhood of Bridge and Fulton streets. The American army rested quietly, not dreaming of the impending danger. Meanwhile the British army was not inactive. It was encamped at Flatbush. Just after midnight it occupied the roads leading to East New York, and pushed forward to that suburban spot. The guides who had been employed lost their way, and General Howe found it absolutely necessary to obtain more trustworthy leaders. In consulting upon the subject, it was determined that William Howard, the keeper of the tavern, being familiar with the different passes, was the best man to secure in the emergency. The approach of the army had not been observed by the occupants of the wayside hotel. Suddenly the bar-room door was forced open, and the terrified family were aroused from their slumbers. The guard sought and found the astonished innkeeper, and quickly brought him before the august generals Howe, Cornwallis, and Sir Henry Clinton. It was their desire to use this man to guide them over the hills and through the woods to the little hamlet at Bedford, where it was supposed a large body of Americans were encamped, whom the invaders desired to outflank, and by a circuitous route, if possible, gain the plain beyond, and thus cut off their rear. Howard was perfectly familiar with the intricate pathways. The interview between Howard and the British officers was brief and to the point. William Howard had a son then only fourteen years of age. The events of the evening left a vivid impression on the lad's mind. In after years, in referring to the adventures of that night, he said: " It was about two o'clock in the morning of the 27th of August that I was awakened by seeing a soldier by the side of my bed. I got up and dressed, and went down into the bar-room, where I saw my father standing in one corner, with three British soldiers before him, with muskets and bayonets fixed. The army (numbering about sixteen thousand men) was then lying in the fields in front of the house. General Howe asked for a glass of liquor, and, after receiving it, entered into conversation with William Howard, and said: 'I must have some one to show me the Rockaway path around the pass.'"

To this remark Howard replied: "We belong to the other side, General, and can't serve you against our duty." General Howe then said: "That is all right, stick to your country, or stick to your principles; but, Howard, you are my prisoner, and must guide my men over the hill." Howard, in the nobility of his nature, objected to being a party to the betrayal of his countrymen, but was silenced by the General, who finally said: "You have no alternative. If you refuse, I shall have you shot through the head."[1]

It was a painful task for Howard to thus pave the way for the destruction of the American army. He was led out under a guard, which was directed to shoot him should he attempt to make his escape. The entire march was conducted in a cautious, noiseless manner, and every precaution taken to be in readiness for an attack. They succeeded in reaching the road below the Bedford pass, and flanked the position supposed to be occupied by the American troops.

[1] *Corporation Manual of Brooklyn*, 1866.

Young Howard, who accompanied his father, in giving an account of the march, says: "On reaching the turn in the Jamaica road, my father and myself were released and sent back to the tavern, which we found surrounded by the guard."

It may be well to state here that the Rockaway path was a narrow pass across the hill, forming now a portion of Evergreen Cemetery, and led from the Jamaica road to Bushwick lane, now the main entrance to the cemetery.

In the legal documents of the time, the roads were called the King's highways. The Brooklyn and Jamaica road, which passed through the hills near East New York, was known as the King's highway. General Howe named it, "the pass through the hills."

The name of the Clove road originated from the fact that it passed through the clove or cleft of the hills. By the British army it was distinguished as the Bedford pass. The valley through which the Flatbush road passed, being densely covered with wood, was called Valley Grove.

The enemy, having crossed over from Long Island and effected a landing in New York city on the 15th of September, immediately pushed forward to meet and drive before them the forces of Washington, which movement on their part culminated in the battle of Harlem Heights. In that engagement, which was short and fierce, the Americans lost, in killed, 16 privates, whilst the damage done to the enemy was 74 killed and 274 wounded. Governor Clinton, who witnessed the battle, wrote of it: "It has animated our troops, given them new spirits, and erased every bad impression the retreat from Long Island had left in their minds. They find that they are able with inferior numbers to drive their enemy, and think of nothing now but conquest."

Shortly after the occupation of New York by the British, and on the 21st of September, the city was visited by a great fire, which quickly reduced a large part of it to ashes. It is estimated that 500 houses were obliterated. Trinity Church was destroyed, and the Lutheran chapel, situated on the corner of Rector Street, met the same fate. St. Paul's Church, the oldest religious edifice now standing in New York city, was saved by the energy and superhuman exertions of the citizens. Long may this old landmark resist the vandalism of the age. The fire was looked upon as the act of an incendiary. The Tory element of the community, believing that it was caused by the Sons of Liberty, accused them of the act. Several citizens were arrested as accessories, but were subsequently discharged, as no evidence could be produced on which to hold them.

During this time the Continental Congress continued to hold its sessions in the city of Philadelphia.

On the 31st of August, Washington sent a letter to Congress wherein he gave an explicit statement of the result of the council of war held on Long Island, and the reasons which led him to withdraw the troops from that locality. By reason of this decision New York city, and all its fortifications, was ultimately given up to the British fleet and army. The new occupants, upon taking possession, adopted measures to fortify and strengthen it against invasion from the American forces.

After the occupation of New York by the British army, large numbers of Tories, who had been compelled to forsake the place by reason of the stringent measures adopted by the Committee of Safety against all who sided with royalty, again returned to the city and were warmly welcomed by the new authorities. Amongst the number who returned to their old haunts was Rivington the printer, whose vituperations against the Sons of Liberty had in former times called down upon him the wrath and enmity of the patriots. The returning Tories held high carnival in the city. They seemed to think that the cause of the Americans was lost, and that soon they would have undisputed control of public affairs.

Kings County, which never had manifested a strong patriotism, contained many who did not greatly lament the triumph of the British. The retreat of the American army from Long Island served to strengthen the convictions of the Tory adherents, and induced them to embrace the opportunity afforded of forsaking what they conceived to be the "lost cause," and give in their adhesion to the Crown of England. Moreover, as we shall see by later explanation, there was a peculiarly heavy pressure placed on the loyalty of Kings County.

It was under this pressure that in November some of the largest freeholders in the county of Kings met together and resolved to accept the terms offered by Howe in his proclamations. In order to gain favor with the British authorities, an address was prepared in the Uriah Heep style, in which it was stated: —

"We, therefore, whose names are hereto subscribed, freeholders and inhabitants of Kings County, in the province of New York, reflecting with the tenderest emotions of gratitude on this instance of his Majesty's paternal goodness and encouraged by the affectionate manner in which his Majesty's gracious purpose hath been conveyed to us by your Excellencies, who have thereby evinced that humanity is inseparable from that true magnanimity and those enlarged sentiments which form the most shining characters, they beg leave to represent to your Excellencies, that we bear true allegiance to our rightful sovereign George the Third, as well as warm affection to his sacred person, crown, and dignity, to testify which we and each of us have voluntarily taken an oath (in the church at Flatbush) before Wm. Axtell, Esq., one of his Majesty's council for this province, in the following words: '*I do solemnly promise and swear that I will be faithful and bear true allegiance to his Majesty King George the Third, and that I will defend his crown and dignity against all persons whomsoever. So help me God.*' And that we esteem the constitutional supremacy of Great Britain over these colonies, and other depending parts of his Majesty's dominions, as essential to the union, security, and welfare of the whole empire; and sincerely lament the interruption of that harmony which formerly subsisted between the parent state and these her colonies. We therefore hereby pray that your Excellencies would be pleased to restore this country to his Majesty's protection and peace." [1]

This was certainly a model epistle, and clearly demonstrated the character of the men who endorsed its sentiments, or pretended to endorse them, by appending to it their names. As the common people had expressed themselves so freely, the leaders, not to be outdone in giving evidence of submission to royalty, a short time afterwards presented to Governor Tryon an address couched in terms of detestation of the rebellion, and of warm admiration for the Crown. It was a craven document, evincing cowardice and lack of true manliness. It ran as follows: —

"We, the members of the Provincial Congress, the County Committee, and the Committees of the different townships, elected by the inhabitants of Kings County, feel the highest satisfaction in having it in our power to dissolve ourselves without danger of the county being dissoluted, as it was by repeated threats

[1] Onderdonk, *Kings County*, sec. 829.

some short time ago. We do hereby accordingly dissolve ourselves, rejecting and disclaiming all power of Congress and committees, totally refusing obedience thereto, and revoking all proceedings under them whatsoever, as being repugnant to the laws and constitution of the British Empire, and undutiful to our sovereign, and ruinous to the welfare and prosperity of this county. We beg leave to assure your Excellency we shall be exceeding happy in obeying the legal authority of government, whenever your Excellency shall be pleased to call us forth, being of long experience well assured of your Excellency's mild and upright administration."

This paper was signed on December 3 and 4. Amongst the parties who appended their signatures to this obsequious missive are the following, many of whom will be recognized as prominent in the annals of the community : —

Philip Nagel	Denyse Denyce
Wm Johnson	Engelbert Lott
Evert Suydam	I. Hubbard
Richard Stillwell	Garret Wyckoff
Johannes E. Lott	Richard Stillwell, Jr.
Rem Cowenhoven	Rutgers Van Brunt
Nich Cowenhoven	Adrien Hegeman
Joost Duryea	Abram Laguare
Jeremiah Vanderbilt	Derick Remsen
Stephen Voorhies	Abram Voorhies

Adrian Voorhies
Petrus Van Pelt
Leffert Lefferts
Wilh⁸ Stoothoof
Casper Crisper
Isaac Cortelyou
Petrus Lott
Johannes De Bevoice

Isaac Denyce
Johannes Bergen
John Vanderbilt
Theodorus Polhemus
Wm Van Brunt
Jacobus Vanderwenter
Cor^s Wyckoff
Jeremias Remsen[1]

That these men, who had served in official stations in councils of the state, and who had witnessed for a dozen years the aggressions of the Crown, should so far submit to British authority, and be willing to resume the yoke when an opportunity was presented by concerted action to throw off the shackles which bound them to the mother country, is perhaps sufficient evidence of the strain produced by the peculiar situation in Kings County.

The militia, who had rendered but little service to the patriots, now followed the example set them by their leaders, and, to gain favor with the British officers, voluntarily raised and contributed the munificent sum of £310 8s towards defraying the expenses of raising and equipping a new battalion to be employed in the service of the Tories. Howe and Tryon rejoiced greatly over these manifestations on

[1] Onderdonk, *Kings County*, sec. 830.

the part of the people of Kings County. Such acts encouraged them greatly in their labors, and led them to suppose that the war was being carried on by a few zealous but hot-headed fanatics, who desired to enrich themselves by a continuance of the rebellion. They believed that they could control the rich, who did not wish to part with their property to be used in a prolonged campaign, and the poor, who did not desire to be separated from their families by compulsory service in the army. General Howe and Governor Tryon, whose position of late years had become merely nominal, gladly accepted these evidences of obedience to their mandates, and were careful to scatter amongst them the assurance that "his Majesty has observed with great satisfaction the effusions of loyalty and affection which break forth in the address of his faithful subjects, upon their deliverance from the tyranny and oppression of the rebel committees; and the proof given by the inhabitants of Kings County of their zeal for the success of his Majesty's measures by so generously contributing towards the expense of raising Colonel Fanning's battalion cannot fail of recommending them to his Majesty's favor."[1]

[1] Onderdonk, *Kings County*, sec. 830.

No one, upon hearing of these manifestations on the part of the people of Kings County, would for a moment wonder that the leaders of the rebellion against kingly authority should at times feel discouraged and disheartened. However, with so many who were faithless, there were some who still were true to the honored cause. The name of Major Barent Johnson, father of the late General Jeremiah Johnson, stands conspicuously amongst those who were not ashamed to acknowledge allegiance to the infant republic. Johnson was ever distinguished as a patriot, and attested his love of liberty, not only by words but also by actions. On every occasion he fearlessly and boldly advocated the revolutionary movement, and was one of the officers of the Kings County militia who would not truckle to power, and who refused "to sell his heritage for a mess of pottage." When the American army retreated from Brooklyn he followed their fortunes, and was encamped with them at Harlem in 1776, and ever testified his love of country by his willingness to serve her in her hour of danger and trial. In the early part of 1777 he was taken prisoner while accompanying the American army to New Jersey. Subsequently he obtained a parole from General Howe through assistance of a brother Mason, and returned to his home in Kings County. He resided on the old farm in the present nineteenth ward of the city, so long known as the residence of General Jeremiah Johnson. He did all he could to aid the American cause. "In order to help on the cause to which he was devoted, he shrank not from personal and pecuniary risks, but suggested loans from friends in his county to the American government, and himself set the example by loaning, first, £700, and afterwards sums amounting to $5000; all the security for which was a simple private receipt, given, too, in times of exceeding peril and discouragement,—a noble and memorable deed."[1]

There were many signs during 1776 that Kings County's disaffection was recognized. At the session of the Provincial Congress held June 21, the subject of preventing Kings County from giving aid to the enemy was discussed, and resulted in the passage of the following resolution:—

Resolved, That it be recommended to the general committee of Kings County, immediately to take effectual measures that all

[1] Rev. Dr. S. R. Johnson's *Memorial Discourse on General Jeremiah Johnson.*

boats and craft in the bay, on the south and southwest sides of said county, be drawn up or on the upland, to such a distance from the water as to prevent as much as possible the disaffected persons in that county from keeping up a communication with the enemy; and that the oars and sails belonging to the said boats and craft be secured in the most effectual manner.

At this session Kings County was represented by Mr. Lefferts and Mr. Polhemus.

On the 10th of August the Provincial Convention (to which name that of the former Congress had been changed), directed that one half of the militia of Kings County and Queens County be "immediately ordered to march and put themselves under the command of the officer commanding the Continental troops on Nassau Island, to be continued in service until the first day of September next, unless sooner discharged by order of this Convention."

The Convention, having received information that the inhabitants of Kings County had determined not to oppose the enemy, thereupon adopted the following resolution: —

Resolved, That a committee be appointed to repair forthwith to said county, and enquire concerning the authenticity of such report, and in case they find it well founded, that they be empowered to disarm and secure the disaffected inhabitants; to remove or destroy the stock of grain; and if they shall judge necessary, *to lay the whole country waste.* And for the execution of these purposes, they are directed to apply to General Greene, or the commander of the Continental troops in that county, for such assistance as they shall want.

The committee appointed in accordance with this resolution consisted of Mr. Duer, Colonel Remsen, Mr. Hebert, and Colonel DeWit.[1]

On the 13th of August the Convention, in pursuance of the resolution passed on the 10th of August, relative to the Kings County militia, appointed Colonel Jeromus Remsen of Queens County, Lieutenant-Colonel Nich⁸ Cowenhoven of Kings County, and Major Richard Thorne of Queens County, as officers of the militia ordered to be drafted from Kings and Queens counties, and placed them under the command of the officer commanding the Continental troops on Nassau Island.

The Convention of Representatives of the State of New York met again on the 21st

---

[1] *Journal of Provincial Convention*, p. 567.

of August. The first subject which engaged its attention was the character of the credentials presented by the delegates from Kings County. The convention, upon examination and due deliberation, came to the conclusion that the same were defective, in that they did not state "whether any, or what power was given to the representatives therein named." Considering that the representatives so elected should be expressly authorized to assist in framing and establishing a new form of government, and thereby give in their adhesion to the independence of America, the Convention ordered that the said Committee of Kings County be immediately informed of said defect, to the end that a new election might be held, whereat delegates clothed with full power in the premises might be returned.

The Convention of Representatives on the 29th of August passed a resolution recommending to the inhabitants of Long Island "to move as many of their women, children, and slaves, and as much of their live stock and grain, to the mainland, as they can," at the same time "assuring them that Convention would pay the expense of moving the same."

There is much significance in the letter of

John Sloss Hobart to the Committee of Safety, dated October 7, 1776, fairly stating the causes which led to the apparent submission of the citizens of Long Island to the British Crown. He shows that the measures adopted were from necessity and not from choice. He says: —

"Upon the retreat of the army from the island they viewed themselves as abandoned by the Convention, and expecting the enemy hourly amongst them, a general removal appeared impracticable; besides, to quit their pleasant habitations, and throw themselves, with their tender connections, upon the charity of an unknown world, was a degree of apathy to which they had not yet arrived. In a fit of despair they laid down their arms, and made an unconditional submission to what they supposed the inquiring army;[1] the people at large being thus brought to terms, they found it less difficult by threats to induce the individuals who had formerly held commissions under the Crown of Great Britain to resume the execution of their offices; being well led into the snare, every measure tended to draw the *net* closer about them. Notwithstanding which, I am, from the best authority, informed that they are accused by Mr. Tryon and his minions of having submitted only the better

[1] So in the original *Journal of Committee of Safety*, p. 671.

to cover their intention of removing, and that, unless the young men do voluntarily take up arms against their country, an inveterate and disappointed soldiery will be let loose upon them. These considerations induce me earnestly to wish that some measure may be taken to induce the people to quit the island, by offering a support to those who cannot maintain themselves — the aged and infirm must be maintained at public expense."

This letter reveals the true condition of affairs, and forcibly states the motives which led the inhabitants of Long Island to submit to the aggressions of the British.

At the session of the Committee of Safety, held on the 26th of November, some of the inhabitants of the State of Connecticut presented claims for expenses incurred in removing stock and the poor inhabitants from Long Island. A committee was therefore appointed to collect and state these accounts, together with the names of the persons bought of, the quantity of stock, and the names of the persons to whom they belonged, together with the place of their present residence, and report the same to the convention of this State as soon as possible.

This subject was again brought to the attention of the Committee of Safety on the 3d of December, 1776. At that meeting the following letter was prepared and signed by the vice-president and transmitted to Colonel H. B. Livingston: —

"SIR, — The Committee of Safety have received accounts from different towns in Connecticutt, with their demands for transporting stock and effects from Long Island. Some are sent in by private persons, as employed by you for that purpose. I am directed to desire you to send me as particular an account as you can of the stock and other effects you have brought off Long Island, with the number of cattle, sheep, and other stock, the names of the persons to whom they belonged, and in what manner the same was disposed of, and to whom; with such vouchers for the same as you have taken. You will likewise inform us of the number of families brought off by your order, with the names of the heads of each family, as far as in your power, with any other particulars you may think necessary respecting the transportation and disposing of the same."

"To COLONEL H. B. LIVINGSTON."

In January, 1777, the American prisoners in New York were paroled and billeted on the inhabitants of Kings County, Congress agreeing to pay a weekly stipend of two dollars for each for board.¹

Colonel Graydon, in his memoirs, presents a very vivid picture of the scenes and incidents connected with the sojourn of the prisoners amongst the island farmers. He says that "the officers of Colonel Mayan's and Colonel Sher's regiments were quartered at Flatbush. He, with another officer, was placed in the house of Jacob Suydam." It was a large house, with many additions erected at different times, with doubtless a strange and weird appearance. He states that "they were civilly received, but that their presence was not welcome to the Low Dutch, who did not like to have their regular habits interfered with. Had they been sure of receiving the two dollars a week, it might have reconciled them. They were, however, a people who seemed thoroughly disposed to submit to any power that might be imposed on them; and whatever might have been their propensities at an earlier stage of the contest, they were now the dutiful and loyal subjects of his Majesty George III. Their houses and beds were clean, but their living was extremely poor. A sorry wash, made up of a sprinkling of Bohea and the darkest sugar

---

¹ Onderdonk's *Revolutionary Incidents*, sec. 832.

on the verge of fluidity, with half-baked bread (fuel being amongst the scarcest articles in Flatbush), and a little stale butter constituted our breakfast. At our first coming a small piece of pickled beef was occasionally boiled for dinner, but to the beef, which was soon consumed, there succeeded *clippers* or clams; and our unvaried supper was supan or mush, sometimes with skimmed milk, but more generally buttermilk blended with molasses, which was kept for weeks in a churn, as swill is saved for hogs. I found it, however, after a little use, very eatable, and supper soon became my best meal. The table company consisted of the master of the house, Mr. Jacob Suydam, an old bachelor; a young man, a shoemaker of the name of Rem Hegeman, married to Jacob's niece, who with a mewling infant in her arms never failed to appear. A black boy, too, was generally in the room; not as a waiter, but as a sort of *enfant de maison*, who walked about and took post in the chimney corner with his hat on, and occasionally joined in the conversation. Rem Hegeman and Yonichy, his wife, gave themselves no airs, nor was harmony with Uncle Jacob ever interrupted but once, when soured a little he made a show of knocking down Lieutenant

Forrest with a pair of yarn stockings he had just drawn from his legs, as he sat in the chimney corner one evening preparing for bed; but moments of peevishness were allowable to our host, for we had been consuming his provisions while he had never seen a penny of our money. The religion of the Dutch, like their other habits, was unostentatious and plain; a simple silent grace before meat prevailed at the table of Jacob Suydam. When we were all seated, he suddenly clapped his hands together, threw his head on one side, closed his eyes, and remained mute and motionless for about a minute. His niece and nephew followed his example, but with such an eager solicitude that the copied attitude should be prompt and simultaneous as to give an air of absurdity to what otherwise might have been very decent."[1]

Graydon refers to the peculiarities of the Dutch in their habits, customs, and manners. One which seemed to strike him with considerable force was the custom of never asking people to " sit down to the table, but to sit ' by.' "

Judging from the Colonel's narrative, the American prisoners must have had a good

[1] Onderdonk's *Incidents of Kings County*, p. 174.

time at Flatbush. Although at times the enforced inactivity was irksome, the prisoners were favored with the presence of many estimable ladies who did much to render their forced stay agreeable.

Meanwhile, the Convention of Representatives held short sessions on the 5th and 6th of December, 1776, and again on the 11th of February, 1777, when they resolved to adjourn to Kingston, which at once became the capital of the State. On the 6th of March, a state constitution was framed, and provision made for a temporary form of government by electing a council of safety. Abraham Ten Broeck, of Albany, was president of the Convention at the time of the passage of these important measures. Theodorus Polhemus was the only member from Kings County at this convention.

In accordance with the resolution passed April 20, 1777, providing for an *ad interim* government, a council of safety was appointed, and the Convention of Representatives was dissolved on the 13th of May, 1777. Owing doubtless to the disturbed condition of affairs in Kings County, that county was not represented in the committee.

The Council of Safety, at its session on the

27th of June, in response to the petition of Obadiah Jones and other refugees from Long Island, reported the following resolutions: —

Resolved, Thereby provided His Excellency Governor Trumbull shall approve thereof, Obadiah Jones, John Hulbart, and Thomas Dearing, or any two of them, do give permits to such refugees from Long Island as reside in Connecticut as they shall think proper, and at such times and under such restrictions as they may judge prudent, to pass to Long Island to get off their effects.

Resolved, That Obadiah Jones, John Hulbart, and Thomas Dearing, or any two of them, be, and they are hereby authorized and directed to remove, at the expense of this state, to the county of Dutchess, within the same, all such refugees from Long Island, now in Connecticut, as are unable to maintain themselves, and are willing so to be removed.

Resolved, That one hundred pounds be advanced to the said gentlemen to enable them to execute the above resolutions; and that they account with the auditor-general of this state for the expenditure thereof.

Ordered, That the treasurer of this state pay the said sum of one hundred pounds unto Mr. Paul Reeve, to be by him conveyed and delivered to said gentlemen or one of them.

Resolved, That the persons so to be removed

shall, on their arrival in Dutchess County, be under the care of and supplied with the necessaries by Mess. Abraham Schenck and Gerlim Van Veelon, commissioners for superintending and providing for such of the inhabitants of this state in the said county as have been driven from their habitations by the enemy.

Kings County was not represented at the first meeting of the new Senate at Kingston in September. In the Assembly which met and organized, William Boerum and Henry Williams represented Kings County. These gentlemen, owing to the peculiar condition of affairs in Kings County, and the impossibility of holding an election, were appointed by the Convention, on May 8th, to represent the county. The members of the Senate and Assembly for the counties of New York, Queens, Suffolk, and Richmond, were appointed in like manner.

The Provincial Convention having instituted the office of auditor-general, for the purpose of settling certain accounts, the appointment to this office was given to Comfort Sands, July 24, 1776, who held the place until March 23, 1782, when he resigned. In 1797 the office was abolished, and that of comptroller was instituted in its place. Comfort Sands, who filled the important position of auditor, deserves more than a passing notice. During his life he took a deep interest in Brooklyn affairs, and owned considerable property in the village. He purchased a part of the property belonging to John Rapalje, whose wife, we have seen, sent her negro servant to apprise General Howe of the premeditated retreat from Brooklyn on the 29th of August, 1776. Rapalje's property extended along the water front from the Ferry to the Navy Yard. He was an influential man, and during colonial times had frequently been a member of the Assembly. When the war commenced in earnest, his family became identified with the Tory element. A bill of attainder was passed against him October 27, 1779, and he was banished. When the British occupied Long Island, he returned to his home, remaining until 1783, when, with his family, he removed to England. His estates having been confiscated, Comfort and Joshua Sands, on the 13th of July, 1784, purchased 160 acres of them, bordering on the East River, for £12,450, paid in state scrip.

It might be well to state here that John Rapalje was clerk of Kings County in 1775, and continued in that office during the British control. His successor, Jacob Sharp, Jr., did not assume the office until 1784. When Rapalje removed to England, he carried with him the town records. These documents were very valuable.

A few years after the declaration of peace Rapalje's granddaughter visited America, hoping to regain possession of her father's land, upon the technical point that the confiscation had taken place subsequent to the treaty of peace. The advice of counsel was taken, whose opinions were adverse to her claim, and she abandoned the effort and returned to Europe. When Mrs. Weldon, the granddaughter, came to America, she brought with her the missing records, and sought to sell and dispose of them for $10,000. The inhabitants looked upon the price as fabulous, and refused to accept the offer. Had they been wise, they would have asserted their rights, and by legal proceedings secured the property, which belonged to the town. By reason of the abstraction of these documents a hiatus has been created in the history, and much valuable information lost. The documents were taken back to England. Even at this late date they probably might be secured from the descendants of the family.

Comfort Sands, who by this purchase became interested in Brooklyn, was born at Sands Point, L. I., in 1748. After serving a clerkship he went into business on his own account in 1769. When he resigned his position as auditor, he resumed business in New York. Having served in the Provincial Congress, at the close of the war he was again called into service. He was a member of the Assembly in 1784–85, 1788, and 1789.

Egbert Benson, of Queens County, was appointed attorney-general by an ordinance of the Constitutional Convention, May 8, 1777. The council of appointment afterwards ratified the act, and on the 15th of January, 1778, granted and issued to him a commission. He filled this responsible trust until May 14, 1789. Egbert Benson was a man of culture. He graduated at Columbia College in 1765. He was a classmate of Robert R. Livingston, with whom he was ever on intimate terms. They served together in the different conventions for the common cause. He was subsequently judge of the New York Supreme Court, and justice of the United States Circuit Court, New York.

The treaty of peace between the American

and British commissioners was signed on September 3, 1783. On November 25, following, the British troops formally evacuated New York and Brooklyn, and the flagstaff of the Pierrepont mansion on the Heights, which had been used for signaling during the battle of Brooklyn, once more floated the American flag.